To Vivian and Anne
with love…

THE MAGNIFICENT 92

Indiana Courthouses

PHOTOGRAPHS BY WILL COUNTS
TEXT BY JON DILTS

ROSE BUD PRESS
PUBLISHERS - BLOOMINGTON, INDIANA

in association with
HARMONY HOUSE, LOUISVILLE

Library of Congress Catalog Number: 91-62669

Hardcover International Standard Book Number: 1-56469-002-4

Printed in Canada

First Edition, October, 1991

Copyright ©1991 by Jon Paul Dilts

Published by Rose Bud Press, P.O. Box 5713, Bloomington, Indiana 47407,
in association with Harmony House, Louisville, Kentucky.

Photographs copyright © 1991 by I. Wilmer Counts

Introduction

By Jon Dilts

Building fancy courthouses may have been the fashion in 1879, but to the aging Lagrange County lawyer, John B. Howe, there was something odd about building a building worth as much as the whole county.

"A courthouse should be like justice itself," he said, "simple and unostentatious, but since it is the fashion to build expensive public buildings, I'll do my part."

Yet the $71,000 price at Lagrange was modest compared with the $150,000 spent at Crawfordsville three years earlier or the $276,000 that went into the courthouse at Vincennes.

Architects were designing new courthouses all over Indiana in a flurry of construction during the last quarter of the 19th century. Thomas Tolan and his son, Brentwood, drew plans for magnificent structures at Fort Wayne, Columbia City, Lagrange, Muncie, La Porte, Rockville and Warsaw. Other architects tried to match the Tolan splendor at places like Crawfordsville and Columbus, Evansville and Frankfort, Terre Haute and South Bend. Even tiny Winamac in rural northern Indiana spent $50,000 and hired A.W. Rush of Grand Rapids to design a splendid limestone building. A year later, Rush designed a courthouse for Rushville with a price five times that of Winamac's -- $257,000.

Cities seemed to compete with one another for splendor and expense. Evansville hired a sculptor from Chicago to create 14 statues of human figures to stand amid limestone carvings of fruits, flowers and vegetables native to southern Indiana. The city hired local artisans to carve the interior woodwork. The cost: $400,000.

This wasn't entirely foolishness. Old courthouses built of wood or brick 30 years before were small and dangerous. Records often had to be stored elsewhere where fire was not such a constant threat. Some counties were so cramped they were renting private offices for employees. New buildings were inevitable.

Not only were they inevitable, but it was acceptable for them to be expensive. There was money. Even in rural areas, there was cash in hand or cash to be borrowed. Some counties raised funds by modest tax levies; others issued bonds to spread the debt over decades. A few paid cash from surplus funds accumulating in the local treasury since the Civil War. A couple were able to raise money by public subscription and private gifts.

And there was motive. It was widely believed that prominent public buildings advertised the success of a community and attracted new business to the local economy. Moreover, Indiana allowed citizens to petition for removal of the county seat, and with removal could come obscurity and financial instability. One loser was Leavenworth in Crawford County, whose status as county seat was moved to English in 1896. English won the prize by offering, among other things, a brand-new courthouse.

But most of all there was fashion. The rich and elaborate Grant and Richardsonian architectural styles were popular in new public buildings in the East -- in Washington, Philadelphia, Pittsburgh and New York. Midwestern architects, with the ability to use native limestone from nearby Bedford quarries, could build with ease those same massive structures they studied and admired. More-over, nothing prevented them from adding their own eclectic flour-ishes. And they did.

About 60 of Indiana's 92 courthouses were built in the 19th century, but the desire to build capitols of grace and grandeur didn't die with the turn of the century.

The years between 1900 and 1930 produced 23 more Hoosier courthouses, most in a classical renaissance style with soaring Greek columns, brilliant stained glass ceilings and richly tiled floors. But with the 1930s came a depression that forever changed Indiana. Only three new courthouses were built in the 1930s, mostly to take advantage of federal assistance aimed at putting builders back to work. None were built in the war years of the 1940s and only one in the 1950s.

By the 1960s and 1970s much of county government in Indiana operated from old, crowded, begrimed buildings dating to the days before World War I. A few counties simply tore them down and rebuilt with a new kind of splendor in glass and steel. But most counties, while intent on building larger facilities, were also intent on keeping and restoring the magnificence they saw in the old build-ings designed by Brentwood Tolan or A.W. Rush or George Bunting. Elaborate, old courthouses were lost at Muncie, New Albany, Logansport and English, but places like Evansville, Fort Wayne, Bloomington, South Bend, Plymouth and Crown Point were able to build new government office buildings while protecting their grand-fathers' Roman and Victorian dreams.

On these pages are the images of those dreams and a glimpse of the people whose lives are still intertwined with the symbols of justice, politics and celebration. Here is the story of Hoosier places where marriages and births and wars and deaths and home-made entertainment are all linked to the courthouse square.

Adams/Decatur

The Adams County Courthouse in Decatur was designed by J.C. Johnson, a self-taught architect who had been trained as a carpenter and a joiner. Yet, he was a gifted designer and won second place in the competition to design the Indiana State Capitol.

Johnson used patterned slate mansard roofs and red brick walls richly ornamented with stone quoins. He originally placed the tower over the courtroom but that worried the commissioners, who were concerned that it was insufficiently supported. In 1898 Wing and Mahurin of Fort Wayne redesigned the tower and placed it above the entrance.

Adams County was the home of the writer and naturalist, Gene Stratton Porter, whose Girl of the Limberlost, written in 1909, was a longtime Hoosier best seller. The Limberlost was a swampy, wild place, and it figured also in a court story about a bailiff who was sent out to find a witness.

To get the witness was a matter of urgency because the jurors had already been selected and were waiting. The out-of-town lawyers were restless and becoming a nuisance, and the judge was cranky. Armed with his warrant, the bailiff rode out after the witness only to return the next day dirty and tired. He had chased the witness into the Limberlost and returned, of course, empty handed. His warrant properly noted the justification for this failure, an excuse recognized by the Adams Circuit Court: the witness was "perceivable but not getable."

A pillory stock stands outside the Adams County Courtroom.

Courthouse built	*1872-1873*
Architect	*J.C. Johnson, Fremont, Ohio*
Construction	*Christian Boseker, Fort Wayne*
Cost	*$78,979*
Population 1990	*31,095*

Sophisticated Corinthian columns grace the doorway of the Adams County Courthouse.

Allen/Fort Wayne

Louis Peltier watched quietly as the cornerstone of the Allen County Courthouse was laid in November 1897. Peltier was the oldest living man in Fort Wayne that year. He could remember when Fort Wayne was actually a fort. Now he watched the placement of a stone that promised to produce a vision, a renaissance revival of architecture and art to mark a American passage into the 20th century.

The Allen County Courthouse, designed by Brentwood Tolan and completed in 1902 at a cost of more than $800,000, was among the finest and most expensive of the new courthouses in Indiana. It was built in a style strongly influenced by classical architectural ideas made popular at the Chicago World's Fair in 1893. Along with the Vanderburgh County Courthouse at Evansville (1887-1890) and the St. Joseph County Courthouse at South Bend (1897-1898), it was an early example of the Beaux Arts renaissance style that suited the academic tastes of formal architecture.

Sculpture, paintings and stained glass were often beyond the budget of a county or were given low priority by architects. So where they do appear, they are notable as statements of economic and social confidence. Fort Wayne was enormously confident at the turn of the century, and that is reflected in the magnificence of a courthouse that was built on the scale of a state capitol. The Allen County budget permitted murals and bas-reliefs in the courtrooms and in the rotunda; it permitted skylights and a central dome of stained glass. The budget for art alone exceeded the cost of many contemporary Hoosier courthouses.

The building now serves primarily as a government annex. Most of the offices were moved in 1971 to a new City-County Building.

A courtroom in the Allen County Courthouse.

Courthouse built	*1897-1902*
Architect	*Brentwood S. Tolan (1855-1923),*
	Fort Wayne
Construction	*James Stewart & Company, St. Louis*
Cost	*$817,553*
Population 1990	*300,836*

An impressive work of interior decoration is the the spectacular dome of the Allen County Courthouse.

The glass interior of the Columbus City Hall frames a portrait of its resplendent cousin, the Bartholomew County Courthouse.

Bartholomew/Columbus

The Bartholomew County courthouse was built in Columbus in the early 1870s in a style sometimes named for General Ulysses S. Grant. The so-called Grant courthouse was typical of the period after the Civil War when Grant was president (1869-1877).

But it was really the Second Empire French, and in particular the Parisians, who popularized the mansard roof among architects in the 1850s. The Americanization of the French style in the 1870s brought new pitches and curves the French hadn't thought about, but most of all it brought towers.

The courthouse at Columbus is part of a collection of period courthouses. Issac Hodgson, who designed the courthouse at Columbus, also built a courthouse with a mansard roof in Henry County at New Castle in 1865-1869, probably the earliest example of mansardic Second Empire style for public buildings in the Midwest.

Some other courthouses of the same style in Indiana include those in Adams County at Decatur (1872-1873) by J.C. Johnson and in Benton County at Fowler (1874) by Gordon P. Randall. There are also those in Lagrange County at Lagrange (1878-1879), Park County at Rockville (1879-1881) and Kosciusko County at Warsaw (1882-1884) all by Thomas J. Tolan. And there are those in Hamilton County at Noblesville (1878-1879) by Edwin May and in Vigo County at Terre Haute (1884-1888) by Samuel Hannaford.

In Columbus, where Hodgson had a whole city block to work with, he decided to place the Courthouse in a corner, allowing its asymmetric L-shaped plan to face two major streets.

Hodgson liked to put inscribed tablets in high positions above doors or on tower walls. At Columbus, rather than putting the inscription naming the commissioners, architect and date on a low cornerstone, he put it on an ornamental parapet centered at the top of the east facade.

Hodgson was born in 1826 at Belfast, Ireland, and came to the United States in 1848. While he lived in Indiana, Hodgson designed six Indiana courthouses.

The Circuit Court judge's bench in Bartholomew County.

Courthouse built	1870-1874
Architect	Isaac Hodgson (1826-1909), Indianapolis
Construction	McCormack & Sweeney, Columbus
Cost	$225,000
Population 1990	63,657

Benton/Fowler

As Indiana moved into the 1870s, the commissioners in Benton County asked G.P. Randall his expert opinion -- he was an architect from Chicago with a contract for a courthouse in Marshall County -- about the condition of the Benton County Courthouse. He told them what he knew they wanted to hear.

"It may not fall down for years," said Randall, "but could give way at any time."

The commissioners eventually hired Randall to replace their old building, which he did in 1874. Randall built a lovely courthouse with a mansard-roofed entrance tower, steep, hip roofs and dormer windows. Randall was known for his Second Empire French style courthouses in Illinois, and his courthouse at Plymouth in Marshall County (1870-1872) was a great success.

But it wasn't just style that commissioners were looking for in the 1870s. It was security. The old courthouses of the 1830s and 1840s were threatened constantly by fire and theft, and they were always too small for large meetings. Arson was not uncommon where the destruction of records could hide crime or confuse a title. These new buildings needed fireproof vaults the size of rooms.

Money, of course, was the catch. Indiana law during the 19th century allowed local government a lot of room to finance public works. Counties were able to tax to create building funds, and they were free to borrow by selling bonds. But the best money was the kind that didn't produce a debt or higher taxes, and so sometimes counties were able to obtain sizable donations in cash or land or equipment from citizens who believed the presentation of the county courthouse made a difference in the local economy.

Private, donated money was rare, but it could be a blessing. Benton County was blessed when Mr. and Mrs. Moses Fowler of Lafayette donated cash for the new courthouse at Fowler.

The Benton County Circuit Courtroom.

Courthouse built	1874
Architect	*Gordon P. Randall, Chicago*
Construction	*Levi L. Leach*
Cost	*$62,257*
Population 1990	*9,441*

Digests of court opinions line the walls of the law library in the Benton County Courthouse.

Blackford /Hartford City

The Blackford County Courthouse, designed by La-Belle & French of Marion, is a good example of an 1890s Romanesque courthouse. It is characterized by rough stonework, bold and massive details, and wide, semi-circular doorways. A major feature is its three-story entrance arches at each end of the building.

The clock tower rises to 165 feet from the corner of the building without breaking the symmetry of the facade below the cornice line, so that it appears to rise from the roof.

The building cost about $130,000 and was influenced by the work of Henry Hobson Richardson, a Boston architect and Harvard graduate who studied at the Ecole des Beaux-Arts in Paris. Richardson died in 1886 at the height of is career, but his influence on American architects was tremendous. Almost all of the Romanesque courthouses in Indiana were built within a decade of his death.

LaBelle and French built one other Romanesque courthouse in Indiana in the mid-1890s. It was at Monticello in White County. Although more modest then the Blackford County version, it was very similar and had an interesting octagonal tower. That White County courthouse was destroyed by a torna-do in 1974 and was replaced by a modern, three-story brick and concrete office building.

Brass chandeliers, painted ceilings and tile wainscoting decorate the hallways in the Blackford County Courthouse.

Courthouse built	*1893-1895*
Architect	*Arthur LaBelle & Burt L. French, Marion*
Construction	*Christian Boseker & Son, Fort Wayne*
Cost	*$129,338*
Population 1990	*14,067*

Floor to ceiling files form a backdrop for Carol Baird and Yvonne Farling in the County Clerk's office at Hartford City.

A winter moon shines in the twilight glow of the Boone County Courthouse.

Boone/Lebanon

Joseph T. Hutton designed the Boone County Courthouse as a capitol building. Hutton had something grander in mind than just the revival of classical Greek styling. This was no simple, neo-classical courthouse nor simply an exercise in academic classicism. It was to be a building for the 20th century, a building with an enormous dome and magnificent limestone pillars.

Hutton's courthouse was so different from its predecessor that the shift in style was nothing short of radical. To make way for the new building, Boone County razed a 1857 Gothic style courthouse, a rarity in Indiana. Gothic touches were sometimes part of the Romanesque buildings of the late 19th century, for example at Knox in Starke County, but truly Gothic styles were confined almost entirely to churches and colleges.

That old Boone County Courthouse (1856-1909) had been a William Tinsley design. Like his Christ Church Cathedral in Indianapolis and his Center Hall at Wabash College, his Boone County Courthouse, with its brick tower and tall, narrow windows, was European and Medieval. It was a fine building and an expensive one ($33,000 in 1856), but it couldn't make a 20th century statement about the secular power of the state.

Hutton's courthouse, on the other hand, was completed in late 1911 at a cost of about $265,000. He used granite and Indiana limestone. The columns were thought to be the largest one-piece limestone columns in the world. There were eight of them, cut from a single piece of limestone 80 feet long. The stone was roughly cut into eight hexagonal shapes about 38 feet long and 4 1/2 feet in diameter for shipment to Lebanon by rail -- one to a car. They were then finished on site and each trimmed to a length of about 35 feet 5 1/2 inches, each weighing about 30 tons.

When in place, they were like nothing that had ever been done in the 19th century.

This colorful Bicentennial quilt celebrates the history of Boone County. It is suspended over the courthouse rotunda.

Courthouse built	1909-1911
Architect	Joseph T. Hutton, Hammond
Construction	Caldwell & Drake, Columbus, Ind.
Cost	$265,000
Population 1990	797,159

Brown/Nashville

In 1873 a fire destroyed the 20-year-old Brown County Courthouse. The replacement was a simple, brick building without pretensions. McCormack & Sweeney of nearby Columbus in Bartholomew County probably designed it.

Although not an architectural firm, the company was experienced at building courthouses. At the time it took the Brown County job, it was working with architect George Bunting on the Montgomery County Courthouse (1874-1876) at Crawfordsville and had just completed Isaac Hodgson's courthouse at Columbus (1871-1874). Those courthouses would cost their local governments 10 to 20 times what the commissioners in Nashville would pay.

What Brown County wanted was a building that was inexpensive in those inflationary times and a building that was solid, useful and straightforward. That is what McCormack & Sweeney gave them. It is a 19th century building without fuss. That in itself gives it a special place among Indiana courthouses. The decade of the 1870s was typically a period of elaborate designs, ornamentation and innovation. Brown County, isolated and rural, nestled in woods and hills, either couldn't compete with the major investors or didn't want to.

Instead, the county built a lovely, brick building where the roads met in Nashville. It didn't even become a town square, just a place to do business, record deeds and seek justice. More than 105 years later, McCormack & Sweeney's building is still there. The frugal commissioner's $9,000 investment (half paid up front and half paid two years after construction at 10 per cent interest) figured out to cost the taxpayers less than $90 a year.

Both because of and in spite of its country ways, Brown County and the county seat at Nashville attract tourists by the bushel.

Courthouse built	1874-1875
Construction	McCormack & Sweeney, Columbus
Cost	$9,208
Population 1990	14,080

Brown County clings to its gentle, country style even when it caters to big city tourists looking for local crafts. This is the view from the courthouse, looking past the pump to the main, downtown intersection.

This Civil War battle scene is a bronze relief on the east side of the "The Color Bearer" monument erected in 1888 on the lawn of the Carroll County Courthouse.

Carroll/Delphi

Elmer Dunlap liked the restrained classical style in courthouse architecture, and he, along with J.W. Gaddis and John Bayard of Vincennes, helped to make it a popular choice all over Indiana.

Dunlap's courthouse at Delphi in Carroll County is a little more ornate than his 1921 version at Rockport in Spencer County, but not by much. He deliberately understated the exterior of both buildings, leaving the emphasis on the temple-like massiveness of the structure.

However, the interior of the Carroll County Courthouse is far more elaborate than the plain exterior would suggest. The building has an open rotunda with a stained glass dome overlooking a colorful mosaic tile floor. Dunlap used 16 marble columns in eight sets of two on the first floor with marble wainscoting, marble door frames and marble stairways. Still, there is a sense of dignified restraint. The columns are topped with simple Doric capitals and the arches are almost flat.

The courthouse is Carroll County's third. The first, built in 1831-1838, was demolished in 1856 to make way for a large, brick courthouse by M.J. McBride of Logansport. That courthouse had large towers at the corners, including a clock tower at the front left of the building.

The bell was saved from the first courthouse and installed in the second where it was used until 1916. It had been a gift of Sheriff Samuel Davis Gresham, who ordered it from Cincinnati sometime around 1836. The plan was to ship it to Lafayette by boat on the Ohio and Wabash rivers and then on to Delphi by wagon. However, the boat sank in the Ohio and the county had to pay to recover it. The 730-pound bell was sold when work began on the Dunlap courthouse but was returned to the county in 1967.

The Carroll County Civil War monument commemorates battles involving Indiana troops.

Courthouse built	1916-1917
Architect	Elmer E. Dunlap, Indianapolis
Construction	A.E. Kemmer
Cost	$250,000
Population 1990	18,809

In front of the Cass County Courthouse are Melissa Montine and her mother, Tanya.

Cass/Logansport

The Cass County Building is a modern, four-story structure erected in 1977-1979 to replace a Greek Revival courthouse that traced it roots to 1842. In 1887-1888, architect John S. McKean of Chicago incorporated the 1842-1844 courthouse into a new building whose design, while completely obscuring the front of the 1844 edition, continued to maintain its Greek Revival styling.

Eighty-nine years later, when the courthouse had become too small and too frail to adequately serve, the county replaced it with a new building typical of the late 20th century. This one houses a complex of county offices, courtrooms and a jail.

The new Cass County Building cost about $1.7 million to construct, although some sources estimate the cost as closer to $3.5 million. In any case, it compares favorably with other Indiana courthouses built in the 1970s: Clark County at Jeffersonville (1970), $5.2 million; Madison County at Anderson (1972-1973), $4 million; White County at Monticello (1975-1976), $2.4 million.

Logansport, at the confluence of the Eel and Wabash rivers, was established in 1828 along with the creation of Cass County. Only two years earlier Lewis Cass had negotiated a treaty with the Potawatomi and Miami tribes to incorporate the area into the United States. The community was named for James John Logan, a Shawnee chief who was killed while fighting for the United States in the War of 1812. The city prospered as a trading center, and it incorporated in 1836 with the arrival of the Wabash and Erie Canal. By 1860 it had become one of the Midwest's largest rail centers.

The clock tower of the Cass County Building bears the clock and bell from the old 19th century courthouse that preceded it.

Courthouse built	*1977-1979*
Architect	*Richard Byers, Muncie*
Construction	*Jack Steinberger Building Systems*
Cost	*$1.7 million*
Population 1990	*38,413*

The Clark County Recorders office.

Clark/Jeffersonville

In Clark County, Karl Postel, an early traveler through the state, remembered the court there as a primitive affair with the parties seated on boards placed across the stumps of trees. His memories date to 1828 when the chief town and seat of the court was Charlestown, a city of 170 houses and 750 inhabitants.

Postel watched with fascination as a defendant slowly pleaded his case before a tribunal of three judges. The defendant rose and shuffled toward the rostrum. He casually bit into an apple and thought for a while about what he was going to say. It was only when the chief judge suggested patiently that he would like to soon go home that the defendant pocketed the half-eaten apple and proceeded with his defense.

Postel was forever left with the image of that apple and the incredible informality of frontier justice it represented.

More than a 164 years later, Clark County's court sits in a much more formal house at Jeffersonville near the Ohio River. It is part of a multi-million dollar complex constructed in 1970 that, as in Indianapolis, brings together city and county offices. Architects Wright, Porteous & Lowe designed the new City-County Building with rows of graceful arches that soar to the roof line, and they set it in a landscaped and paved plaza with broad, open spaces.

Only about a third of Indiana's 92 courthouses have been replaced in the 20th century and only about eight of those since 1937. There were no courthouses built in the 1940s and only one in the 1950s. Besides Jeffersonville (1970), the past half-century has produced new courthouses at English (1957), New Albany (1961), Indianapolis (1962), Muncie (1969), Anderson (1973), Monticello (1976) and Logansport (1979).

Some counties, as at Vanderburgh, Lake, Allen, St. Joseph and Monroe, have built new office complexes for county government, but they have done that without razing historic courthouses in the process.

Jeffersonville and other Indiana cities began in the late 1960s to put city and county offices in the same government buildings.

Courthouse built	1970
Architect	Wright, Porteous & Lowe
Construction	F.H. Wilhelm
Cost	$5.2 million
Population 1990	87,777

A jet fighter, now more than 35 years old, stands at parade rest in the shadows of the Clay County courthouse.

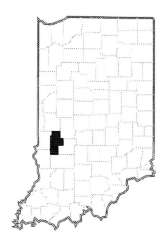

Clay/Brazil

In 1914, when Indiana Governor Samuel M. Ralston dedicated the new Clay County Courthouse in Brazil, he thought the building represented a departure from the confusion of the past to a new and higher order of life.

"A stranger to our civilization," he said, "gazing upon it and beholding the orderly procedure therein contemplated would not fail to note the advanced position you hold in society."

When the County Commissioners contracted with John W. Gaddis in 1912 to design a new courthouse, the trend in architectural styling was already very different from what it had been 10 years before. The new courthouses of the 20th century were to be monuments rather than fortresses. The new taste for the old classical and renaissance styles was producing capitols with great pediments atop tall, stone pillars. Gaddis' early 20th century design reflects the kind of academic correctness and order that would dominate Hoosier courthouses for the next 20 years.

He designed Clay County's with a broad rotunda, inlaid tile floors, marble wainscoting, granite columns towering to the roof and an arched dome of stained glass.

The Gaddis courthouse in Clay County replaced one that had been built in 1873-1876 on land donated two years earlier by Robert and John Stewart. The county seat had been officially moved in 1877 to Brazil when the records were surreptitiously taken from the courthouse at Bowling Green. The courthouse there, built in 1853, languished as a public meeting house until struck by lightening in 1910. Only the steps remain.

In addition to Brazil, Gaddis built courthouses at Greencastle (1903-1905) and Huntington (1904-1906).

The Clay County Courthouse rotunda.

Courthouse built	*1912-1914*
Architect	*John W. Gaddis (1856-1931),*
	Vincennes
Construction	*Baily & Koerner, Louisville*
Cost	*$225,000*
Population 1990	*24,705*

Clinton/Frankfort

George Bunting designed three county courthouses in the 1880s in a style sometimes referred to as county capitol. It grew easily from the earlier Greek Revival and later would merge just as easily into the academic classicism at the beginning of the century. Bunting and other architects looked to classical elements -- especially Italian -- and to state capitols (and the United States Capitol) for models.

Bunting's county capitols were at Franklin in Johnson County (1881-1882), Anderson in Madison County (1882-1885, replaced in 1972) and Frankfort in Clinton County (1882-1884). These were among eight courthouses by Bunting built in a variety of styles, including Romanesque and Second Empire buildings.

By the standards of the 1880s, the Clinton County Courthouse was expensive. In approaching the $200,000 mark it was nearly four times the price of Lake County's courthouse and three times the cost of courthouses in Lagrange County or Wabash County, all built about 1879. But Clinton County wasn't alone in spending big money. In 1880 Grant County built a courthouse at Marion at a cost of about $200,000, and in a few years both Vigo County (1884) and Vanderburgh County (1888) would begin construction of courthouses at a cost of a half million dollars.

Indiana courthouses were paid for in a variety of ways: selling bonds, by special property tax levies, and sometimes by using accumulated tax surpluses. Occasionally, courthouses were built with private donations, as was the case in Benton, Perry and Hamilton counties. In Clinton County, however, construction began with money set aside in an annual courthouse tax levy that began in 1877. The levy was 10 cents on each $100 of assessed property value. After 1882 that rate increased to 20 cents.

That built a three-story, Indiana limestone building, adorned with statuary and distinguished by a remarkable central tower and clock rising to 165 feet.

This is one of a number of sculptured figures that gaze over Frankfort from the top of the Clinton County Courthouse.

Courthouse built	1882-1884
Architect	George W. Bunting (1829-1901), Indianapolis
Construction	Charles Pearce, Indianapolis
Cost	$179,450
Population 1990	30,974

(Opposite) Arts and crafts outside the Clinton County Courthouse.

Crawford/English

Probably the least pretentious courthouse in Indiana is in Crawford County in English. Built during the 1950s the single-story brick structure is largely unadorned.

It replaced an elaborate courthouse built in 1895, a year before English became a county seat. That fancy, old courthouse had been one of the reasons English became a county seat at all. Until then, local government had been at Leavenworth near the Ohio River. County seats in the 19th century could be moved by a petition of the voters. In 1896 English had the petition, a new building, and a court order won after a three-day trial at Corydon, affirming the move to English.

The court order was important because the county records were at the courthouse in Leavenworth, a community unhappy about the move. To get the records, A.J. Goodman led a procession of 96 wagons, 82 mounted guards and 478 infantry to Leavenworth. They left English at 1 a.m., arrived at Leavenworth six hours later, and spent the rest of the day loading and moving material to the new county seat.

The English courthouses is situated at the edge rather than the center of the city. One reason for that was the lateness at which English rose to county seat status. The town began to grow with the arrival of the railroad in 1884, and it was 10 years later that the town became a county seat. The first courthouse was the 1895 edition, and it was built at the center of activity -- near the railroad.

The Crawford County Courthouse, at upper left, is unusual in that it was originally located away from the town center.

Courthouse built	*1958-59*
Architect	*Lester Rauth, Vincennes*
Cost	*$105,851*
Population 1990	*9,914*

This Indian head sits on the judge's bench in Crawford Circuit Court. The seal of the county hangs on the wall.

The balcony and interior colonnades were restored after fire damaged the Daviess County Courthouse in 1986.

Daviess/Washington

On August 27, 1927, fire destroyed Daviess County's 1879 courthouse, designed by George W. Bunting of Indianapolis. Bunting was a prolific architect whose courthouses still stand at Crawfordsville, Franklin, Frankfort, Bloomfield, Bluffton and Liberty.

With the loss of the Bunting courthouse, the county rebuilt in the new style of many early 20th century courthouses in Indiana. It emphasized a simplicity and massiveness that highlights the native limestone. At Washington, a major feature of the design is a powerful and dominant entrance graced by six hugh columns topped with Ionic capitals.

An arsonist heavily damaged the building in 1985, destroying the courtrooms and nearby offices on the second floor. Reconstruction costs ran to more than $500,000. An arsonist in 1891 also had attempted to burn Bunting's Daviess County Courthouse. Repairs then cost somewhat less, about $5,000.

On the courthouse lawn is one of literally hundreds of Civil War monuments in Indiana. This one dates to 1913 and picks up a favorite image of the war: The Color Bearer. Another fine example of The Color Bearer is on the lawn of the Carroll County Courthouse in Delphi.

This monument was erected in 1913 for the 2,312 Daviess County men who fought for the Union Army in the Civil War.

Courthouse built	*1928-1929*
Architect	*Sutton & Routt, Vincennes*
Construction	*English Brothers,*
	Champaign, Illinois
Cost	*$317,136*
Renovation	*1985, $570,000*
Population 1990	*23,717*

Dearborn/Lawrenceburg

Courthouses touch people's lives at critical points: at birth, marriage, war, first mortgages and death. When Judge Lester Baker died on July 7, 1985, he was Indiana's senior jurist and had been on the Dearborn Circuit bench for 36 years.

Judge Baker's life animated a building that was already 76 years old when he became circuit judge in 1949. It was 112 years old when his friends carried his flag-draped coffin into the silence of the courthouse.

Judge Baker's home for all those years was an extraordinary example of post-Civil War architecture. It is a very late example of a 19th century Greek Revival style that eventually merged into the academic classicism at the end of the century.

When the commissioners asked George Kyle to design a new courthouse, they wanted it to be like the fine Greek Revival capitol down river at New Albany. They wanted Corinthian columns and porticoes and classical proportions. Although New Albany's courthouse was built just after the Civil War (1865-1867), it reflected the ante-bellum identification of the classical Greek with the romantic refinements of civilization and power.

That is what the Dearborn commissioners wanted: a place connected with the best of the civilized past, and that is what Kyle was determined to give them.

The Dearborn County Courthouse.

Courthouse built	*1870-1873*
Architect	*George Kyle, Vevay, Ind.*
Construction	*Thomas J. Shannon, Lawrenceburg*
Cost	*$135,775*
Population 1990	*38,835*

Dearborn Circuit Court Judge Lester Baker's funeral in the courthouse rotunda, 1985.

Decatur/Greensburg

Twenty years before Edwin May designed the Indiana State House, he drew the plans for a Decatur County Courthouse in Greensburg.

The building is unusual because it is essentially a Gothic structure with Norman, round-arched windows. Although Gothic Revival was a major stylistic movement of the 19th century and one endorsed by Robert Dale Owen, it generally had little impact on courthouse design in Indiana. May's avoidance of pointed arches at Greensburg reflects the Hoosier ambivalence about a style some believed was more suited for churches or homes. Yet, May used Gothic devices effectively in his courthouses at Greensburg and Vincennes (1872-75), and there are Gothic touches in Starke County (Wing & Mahurin, 1897-1898), and Jasper County (Alfred Grindle, 1896-1898), although neither was a predominately Gothic building.

But it is not architecture for which the Decatur County Courthouse is best known. It is a tree that grows at the top of the 115-foot clock-tower. It was in 1870 that a local citizen first noticed the tree -- a large-toothed Aspen. Since then, many Aspens have grown on the tower roof and have been the subject of ditties and prayers and even pictured in advertisements. In 1884, D. Eckley Hunter wrote of the trees:

"May God bless the angels, and God bless the men
Who plant for a future hour.
And God bless the shade of the maples, and then
The grove on the top of the tower."

May had between $30,000 and $40,000 to spend on the building, but the actual cost, including landscaping and iron fences and last-minute changes, probably came closer to $120,000.

In 1888-1890, the courthouse was extensively remodeled and enlarged. The courtroom was divided into two floors and the first floor was made into county offices. In 1903, the pink brick and limestone trim was covered with stucco to make it look like rock-faced masonry.

Doris Gay works at the desk in the Treasurer's office. A 1882 lithograph of the Decatur County Courthouse decorates the wall.

Courthouse built	1854-1860
Architect	Edwin May (1824-1880), Indianapolis
Cost	$120,000
Addition	1888-1890
Restoration	1977, $300,000
Population 1990	23,645

Decatur County's famous tree grows from the courthouse tower.

Dekalb/Auburn

The DeKalb County Courthouse in Auburn is a fine example of the use of Bedford limestone. The Fort Wayne architectural firm, Mahurin & Mahurin, used it in Auburn to construct a capitol with strong, classical Greek features, including Ionic columns and pediments.

The availability of vast quarries of Indiana limestone had a tremendous impact on the construction of early 20th century government buildings in Indiana. And a good railroad system made it practical to move the stone from southern Indiana to locations throughout the state and the nation.

Between 1905 and 1914, limestone courthouses similar to the one at Auburn were built all over the state: At Greencastle in 1905, Huntington in 1906; Bloomington and Williamsport in 1908; Peru in 1910; Spencer and Lebanon in 1911; and Brazil and Danville in 1914. All the courthouses were built in a similar, classical renaissance style, although few were designed by the same architect.

The style lasted through the 1920s and the construction of about a half dozen more buildings in southern Indiana. But after 1930, when Lawrence County completed a Bedford limestone courthouse in Bedford, the Depression brought a virtual end to limestone courthouses in the classical style. The materials of preference shifted to glass and steel and granite, and the style of preference, beginning with Kokomo in 1936, shifted to new forms belonging exclusively to the 20th century.

Fine old cars parade past the Dekalb County Courthouse each summer during the Auburn-Cord-Duesenberg Festival at Auburn.

Courthouse built	*1911-1914*
Architect	*Mahurin & Mahurin, Fort Wayne*
Construction	*J.B. Goodall, Peru*
Cost	*$317,072*
Population 1990	*35,324*

This mural, framed in marble and called "The Spirit of Industry," was painted by Arthur Thomas in 1913.

THE SPIRIT OF INDUSTRY

THE CENTER GROUP, A SITTING FEMALE FIGURE ALLEGORICAL OF THE
HER RIGHT HAND RESTING UPON THE CONSTITUTION AND HER LEF
SEAL OF THE STATE, GIVING PROTECTION TO AGRICULTURE AND
COUNTY, ASSISTED AND COUNSELED BY A MALE FIGURE ALLEG
EMPLOYES OF THE HUMAN MIND, AT THE BASE OF THE GR
EDUCATION, A WOMAN TEACHER INSTRUCTING A PUPI
MANUFACTURES ARE PORTRAYED AND ON THE
A GREAT FIELD OF GOLDEN WHEAT WITH
FOREGROUND, COWS AND SHEEP, IMPOR

A glass wall opens up the interior of the Delaware County Courthouse to the courthouse plaza.

Delaware/Muncie

In 1969 Delaware County completed a new County Building, replacing an 1887 courthouse designed by Brentwood Tolan. The old courthouse had fallen into ill-repair, and regardless of its historical interest, was too crowded, inefficient and crumbling to be saved.

Joseph Douglas, the County Council President in 1965, remarked that only "a few farmers and older citizens" were opposed to razing the Tolan building and replacing it. Thousands of citizens signed a petition for a new building, responding to an organized effort that included billboard promotions and newspaper revelations of the horrid condition of the building

Architect C. Eugene Hamilton said the new courthouse would represent no particular architectural period or style. The county needed something functional, and that was what this building was intended to be.

Still, the new building was constructed with a sense of style and grace that even Tolan might have found interesting. It is a sweeping three-story structure that flanks two sides of a paved and landscaped plaza. It is constructed of quartz in concrete panels trimmed with granite, and the second and third floors are cantilevered seven feet over the first floor. The building provides 81,000 square feet, more than three times the floor space of the Tolan courthouse.

It is dramatically unlike its predecessor. While Tolan's courthouse was ornate, this one is simple. But then not even Tolan built another courthouse like the one at Muncie. After that project, he began to work on the courthouses at LaPorte, Columbia City and Fort Wayne, making a clear shift in his own architectural tastes.

Three large, carved figures, including this Indian, were salvaged from the exterior of the old Delaware Courthouse.

Courthouse built	*1966-1969*
Architect	*Hamilton, Graham Associates and*
	George W. Cox, Muncie
Construction	*F.A. Wilhelm*
Cost	*$2.4 million*
Population 1990	*119,659*

Dubois/Jasper

The problem with Dubois County in the early 19th century was that it was almost impossible to get anywhere. The area was mostly forest and swamp. The county seat in 1818 was Portersville on the White River just north of the Buffalo Trace. That is where the first official courthouse was, but it wasn't called a courthouse. It was called a Clerk and Recorders Office, even though the real clerk's office was housed in an entirely separate building.

Most people in Dubois County didn't live in Portersville. They lived in clearings in the woods between the White and Patoka rivers. To get to Portersville was not easy. There were neither roads nor bridges -- just trails. Court hearings meant several days away from home.

By 1830, there were about 50 people living in Portersville and about 1,774 people scattered in the northwest corner of the county. Some of those who lived west of Portersville and others who lived near the Patoka River argued for a more central location for the county seat. They had in mind a place where an Indian trail left the Buffalo Trace and crossed the Patoka at a ford -- the only reliable ford on the river.

Because of that ford and the trail and its central location, Jasper became the county seat in 1830. Within the decade, the town had 150 people, a courthouse and a bridge.

That old courthouse burned in 1839 along with all the records and was replaced by a brick courthouse built by a priest, Father Joseph Kundeck.

By the turn of the century, Father Kundeck's Greek Revival courthouse was thought to be too small, and its detractors called it an old-fashioned shack. So, with a new tax levy, the commissioners in 1909 hired a firm of Washington, D.C., architects to replace it.

What they built is a classic renaissance style building with Ionic capitals atop columns that rise to the roof line. It has four stories, reaching to 100 feet, with three porticoes and four entrances.

A soldier stands in relief on an unusual "doorway" on a Civil War memorial near the Dubois County Courthouse.

Courthouse built	*1909-1911*
Architect	*Milburn, Heister & Co.,*
	Washington, D.C.
Construction	*William F. Stillwell, Lafayette*
Cost	*$62,179.00*
Population 1990	*36,616*

Two Dubois County men chat on the street outside the county courthouse.

*Just big enough to see over the railing, Frances Marie Hendry
watches the world from the balcony of the Elkhart County Courthouse.*

Elkhart/Goshen

Shortly after the Civil War, the Elkhart County Commissioners agreed to build a courthouse "appropriate to the progress and standing of the county." They contracted with the Chicago architectural firm of Barrows and Garnsey, who built a brick and stone, two-story building, 82x72 feet. They also built an imposing clock tower at the south end twice the height of the main building.

About 35 years later, the building was extensively remodeled. The tower was razed, the main structure was lengthened at both ends, and a new, domed tower was built over the center of the building. The asymmetrical design of the 19th century changed to a classic capitol style emphasizing symmetry and grace.

To spend more than $100,000 on a two-story-with-basement public building in 1868 was a mark of considerable affluence. Steuben County, for example, in 1868 built a courthouse for about $27,000 and four years earlier both Switzerland and Ripley counties built courthouses for under $30,000. Elkhart County, in its bid to build something appropriate, may have been only the second county in Indiana to spend so much money for a courthouse. Two year's earlier, Henry County completed an Isaac Hodgson designed building for $120,000. A year after Elkhart County completed its work, Marshall County built a G.P. Randall design for about $110,000. The 1880s and 1890s would see prices soar dramatically, but in the 1860s, a $100,000 courthouse was worth a buggy ride to town.

This cast bronze of the Greek god, Poseidion, poses with his trident outside the Elkhart County Courthouse.

Courthouse built	*1868-1871*
Architect	*J.H. Barrows & George O. Garnsey, Chicago.*
	(Firm became Barrows & Barton in 1868)
Construction	*Elkhart County*
Cost	*$124,881*
Renovation	*1904-1906*
Population 1990	*156,198*

This large American flag, painted on concrete, is in tribute to those who have served in the Armed Forces.
It lies in front of the Fayette County Courthouse. The yellow wreath recalls those who served in Operation Desert Storm.

Fayette/Connersville

'In 1890, architects W.F. Kaufman, James McLaughlin, and George Bunting were each designing and building courthouses in the Romanesque style. Kaufman was in Connersville, McLaughlin in Richmond and Bunting in Bluffton and Liberty.

The popularity of these massive buildings in the 1880s and 1890s has left Indiana with a collection of 15, all dating to the same period and representing the work of 11 different architects. Examples can be found in Hartford City, Connersville, Rochester, Greenfield, Rensselaer, LaPorte, Albion, Winamac, Rushville, Knox, Tipton, Liberty, Salem, Richmond and Bluffton.

The courthouse at Connersville in Fayette County is unusual in that it has two front entrances separated by a broad gabled mass. In the gable is a Romanesque version of a Venetian window with heavy lintels. The cylindrical clock tower at the left corner originally had a conical roof. The courthouse is built of brick, and the only other example of a brick, Romanesque courthouse in Indiana is at Albion in Noble County, completed in 1889.

One of the great advantages of the Romanesque style was that it provided large, fire-proof space but still could be adapted to limited budgets. The Fayette County Courthouse was the basic model at just over $36,000. The average cost of a Romanesque courthouse in the 1890s was typically closer to $120,000.

Carved, wooded stairways are less common in courthouses than one might expect. Builders preferred iron or brass because the metals couldn't feed a courthouse fire.

Courthouse built	*1890-1891*
Architect	*W.F. Kaufman, Richmond, Ind.*
Construction	*Dorrus Ready & Co.*
Cost	*$36,192*
Population 1990	*26,015*

Floyd/New Albany

Local government for Floyd County and New Albany is housed in a modern City-County Building overlooking the Ohio River. It was constructed in 1959-1961 at a cost of about $2.4 million. A number of old buildings, including a city hall, jail, Schribner High School and an 1867 courthouse were replaced to make room for the new complex and for a new federal government building.

In 1953 the Indiana General Assembly passed legislation permitting local governments to empower a committee to issue revenue bonds for needed public buildings. Floyd County and New Albany were among the first to use that power to create a new government complex. This became Indiana's first city-county building, and it was followed shortly by Marion County's City-County Building in Indianapolis, built at a cost of about $25 million in 1960-1962.

When the old 1867 courthouse was razed in 1961, the county saved four Corinthian columns from the courthouse and erected them on the north side of the building where they stand in sharp contrast to the starkness of the new structure.

The seal of Floyd County hangs on the face of the City-County Building in New Albany.

Courthouse built	*1959-1961*
Architect	*Walker, Applegate, Oakes & Ritz*
Construction	*Leo C. Miller Company*
Cost	*$2.4 million*
Population 1990	*64,404*

Early morning sunlight highlights one of the Ohio River bridges to Louisville behind the City-County Building.

Fountain/Covington

The courthouse at Covington was built during the Great Depression after the old 1859 building designed by Issac Hodgson was condemned as unsafe. It was one of a number of public works projects that produced fine public buildings in Indiana during those years, including at least two courthouses, this one for Fountain County and another for Shelby County (1936-1937).

Nationally, nearly 600 airports and 110,000 public buildings were built or rebuilt between 1935 and 1941. Other projects included more than a half-million miles of roads and streets and more than 100,000 bridges. It also included thousands of photographs and paintings.

Of particular note at the Fountain County Courthouse are the murals painted by Eugene Francis Savage and others between 1937 and 1940. Savage, born in Covington in 1883, was acclaimed as an American artist during the 1920s and 1930s and taught painting at Yale University from 1923 to 1958. Besides Covington, his work in murals and mosaics can be seen in buildings in Hawaii, Indianapolis, Harrisburg, Pa., Albany, N.Y., and Epinal, France.

The paintings at Covington depict the discovery, settlement and development of western Indiana. Savage directed local artists in producing the murals and, while in New York, personally painted the panels for the entryway. The murals cover more than 2,500 square feet of wall space and in 1971 were appraised at a figure just below the original construction cost of the entire courthouse.

Another example of courthouse murals painted during the 1930s are those of Carl Reinbold in the Jackson County Courthouse at Brownstown.

Fountain County Deputy Recorder, Patti Smith, works behind the counter in the Fountain County Courthouse.

Courthouse built	*1936-1937*
Architect	*Louis R. Johnson & Walter Scholar, Lafayette*
Construction	*Jacobson Brothers, Chicago*
Cost	*$246,734*
Population 1990	*17,808*

The Murals in the Fountain County Courthouse were painted under the direction of Eugene Francis Savage between 1937 and 1940. Savage was born in Covington and achieved great success as an American artist during the 1920s and 1930s.

The courthouse tower rises above traffic on U.S. 52 through downtown Brookville.

Franklin/Brookville

Court was in session in the Franklin County Courthouse on Oct. 13, 1877, when the judge heard the cracking. There was only time to shout a warning and move toward the wall as the roof crashed into the courtroom. Judge Henry Hanna remembered trying to get to the door, and he remembered being blocked by a big man equally intent on getting out.

Across the street at the newspaper office, the editor of the Brookville *American* heard the noise and looked at his watch. It was 9:40 a.m., a Saturday morning. He watched the dust rise from the courthouse and headed for the building.

About 20 people were in the courtroom when the roof collapsed, and several workmen, who had been on the roof, rode down with it. Injuries were limited to cuts and bruises.

Earlier that summer, the commissioners had decided to remodel the old courthouse, built in 1852 by architect Edwin May. They didn't like the flat roof, for one thing. And they didn't like the battle walls nor the tower. So about 18,000 bricks were hauled to the roof to begin work on replacing the flat roof with a mansard version. The weight of those bricks, stacked on the roof, was more than the building could take.

Although the court had to move temporarily, the building was remodeled that year with a new tower and roof. However, the essential lines of May's courthouse with its row of high arches across the front remained until 1910 when the commissioners ordered a second major remodeling.

This time, on the advice of Indianapolis architect Elmer Dunlap, the building was enlarged and incorporated into a classically styled building but keeping the 1852 tower. The courthouse was flanked by wings and given a new front that radically altered its appearance.

Dunlap's courthouse in Brookville, while removing all visible vestiges of the 1850s, retained something of the spirit of the 1870s in the retention of the tower and in the use of brick, rather than limestone.

The Franklin County Courthouse in Spring

Courthouse built	1910-1912
Architect	*Elmer E. Dunlap, Indianapolis*
Construction	*J.W. Millikan, Indianapolis*
Cost	$71,000
Population 1990	19,580

Fulton/Rochester

A.W. Rush's three Indiana courthouses at Rochester, Winamac and Rushville were basically alike -- all Romanesque designs. All three were built of rock-faced limestone with central towers. But the details varied significantly depending on the available financial resources of the counties.

For example, at Rochester the Fulton County Courthouse included semi-circular apses with conical roofs flanking the entrance arch, something that wasn't done at Winamac a year earlier. But then Fulton County's budget for a courthouse was nearly twice that of Pulaski County's. Rush County's budget, on the other hand, was twice that of Fulton County's, and accordingly, it is the most elaborate of the three.

The courthouse at Rochester cost about $100,000. But the basic cost of construction was never the total cost of a public building. The finishing touches, changes and additions could add substantially to the price. Furniture, removal of the trees and grading of the lawn, new walkways and other incidentals brought the real cost in Fulton County to about $125,000. Then changes in the plan of the steps, the decision to use marble along the inside walls and stone coping around the yard, the redesign and rebuilding of the courtroom ceiling for acoustical reasons, the decision to use a more expensive clock than was originally planned and the addition of carved lions to decorate the entrances brought the overall cost to something closer to $200,000.

The stone lions not only added to construction costs but were unusual for a Romanesque building, often notable for a lack of statuary. However, the commissioners were interested in having Rush design dramatic approaches to a dramatic courthouse. Accordingly they authorized the removal of all the large, old oak and maple trees from the grounds so they couldn't detract from the grandeur of the building. Then they commissioned the crouching stone lions to be carved by hand on location. Two lions were to flank the steps at each entrance and others were to be centered in the approach steps.

A stone lion stands guard in front of the Fulton County Courthouse.

Courthouse built	1895-1896
Architect	A. William and Edwin A. Rush,
	Grand Rapids, Michigan
Construction	Jordan E. Gibson, Logansport
Cost	$99,334
Renovation	1975-1976, $600,000
Population 1990	18,840

(opposite) The Fulton County Courthouse is framed by a nearby porch.

Gibson/Princeton

Journalists know the Gibson County Courthouse for the sensational 1955 trial of Leslie Irvin and the subsequent U.S. Supreme Court decision reversing Irvin's conviction because of prejudicial publicity. The jurors had seen enough in the Evansville papers to be convinced that Irvin (the press called him Mad Dog Irvin) had murdered six people in and near Evansville. They found him guilty and sentenced him to death.

On appeal, the press got a stern warning, and Irvin got a new trial. At the second trial, even without the glare of publicity, Irvin was convicted again. The judge sentenced Mad Dog Irvin to life in prison.

The courthouse was 70 years old when Irvin stood trial the first time. It was built in the mid-1880s, and at that time few in Princeton had seen a building so tall or so large. Architects variously classify it as County Capitol or Romanesque Revival. In any case, it is an excellent example of how late 19th century architecture could draw upon a variety of traditional styles and detail to create a statement about the importance of local government. In this building there were Corinthian capitals, Roman arches, decorative terra cotta, ornate carvings and vermiculated limestone.

The interior design made extensive use of black walnut and oak trim, plaster reliefs, mosaic tile floors and brass railings.

Fire protection was a particular concern. So the building used a fireproof floor construction of masonry vaulting, spanning between small iron beams. Four wells on the town square provided water for cisterns and for the steam boilers used to heat the building.

The Gibson County Courthouse was one of 10 built during the 1880s in Indiana that still stand. Others include courthouses in the cities of Albion (1887-1889), Bloomfield (1885-1886), Frankfort (1882-1884), Franklin (18881-1882), Lafayette (1881-1885), Rockville (1879-1881), Salem (1886-1888), Terre Haute (1884-1888) and Warsaw (1882-1884).

Wilma Jean Dossett Rees searches through the hand-written ledgers at the Courthouse looking for clues to the Dossett family's history.

Courthouse built	1883-1885
Architect	Harry, Roy and Kenneth McDonald, Louisville
Construction	Joseph G. Miller
Cost	$118,661
Population 1990	31,913

The names of military veterans are a common feature of Indiana courthouses, as here in Gibson County.

The Grant County Courthouse, now more than a century old, once had a dome that rose 40 feet from the roof.

Grant/Marion

E.E. Myers was rapidly developing a national reputation in the late 1870s when Grant County asked him to design a capitol for the county. His stature was such that by 1883, he would be one of five architects asked to submit designs for the Allegheny County buildings in Pittsburgh, the competition which was won by Henry Hodson Richardson with his trend-setting Romanesque design.

Myers' building in Marion was very different from Richardson's Romanesque in Pittsburgh. Myers wanted it built to look like a capitol rather than a fortress. He used limestone backed by brick and a classical styling that was not exactly Greek Revival and not yet academic classicism.

The massive and stately building may perhaps have seemed a bit old-fashioned (or a bit avant-guarde) in the days after the Civil War when tastes were running toward the Romanesque and the Second Empire, styles that would take center stage during the 1880s and 1890s.

The building's dome, which rose 40 feet above the roof, was removed after a fire in 1943.

With the precinct map are Grant County Republican registrar Billie Jean Hickam (left) and her Democrat counterpart, Ethel Connors.

Courthouse built	1880
Architect	E.E. Myers
Construction	Hinsdale-Doyle Granite Co.
	and W.D. Richardson
Cost	$212,776
Population 1990	74,169

Greene/Bloomfield

Bloomfield's Greene County Courthouse is one of six still standing in Indiana designed by George W. Bunting of Indianapolis. A seventh courthouse, at Washington (1877-1879), was replaced in 1929, and an eighth, at Anderson (1882-1885), was replaced in 1973.

Bunting, with his son, George Jr., built courthouses in places as widespread as Ann Arbor, Mich., Clarkesville, Tenn., Clarksburg, W.Va. and Wichita, Kan. In Indiana, they built courthouses at Crawfordsville (1874-1876), Washington (1877-1879), Franklin (1881-1882), Frankfort (1882-1884), Anderson (1882-1885), Bloomfield (1885-1886), Bluffton (1889-1891) and Liberty (1890-1891).

Bunting was college trained and had been a colonel in the Confederacy during the Civil War. After the war, he moved north to Bloomington, Illinois, where his son was born, and in 1874 was in Indianapolis with the firm of Bunting & Huebner. In the mid-1880s the firm became George W. Bunting & Son and he became one of the state's leading architects.

Besides courthouses, Bunting was known for his buildings on the Indiana University campus at Bloomington. He designed Owen, Wylie, Mitchell and Maxwell Halls. His Greene County Courthouse is in much the same tradition as some of those university buildings and is far less pretentious than many of his other courthouses.

A silent gun is raised in salute to the Green County men and women who have served their nation in war and peace.

Courthouse built	1885-1886
Architect	George W. Bunting (1829-1901), Indianapolis
Construction	McKay & Bushman
Cos	$60,800
Population	30,410

*At the Greene County Courthouse Hoosiers can get married, pay their taxes,
sue their neighbor, and buy a pumpkin, Or, they can sit and talk, or just sit.*

The Hamilton County Courthouse.

Hamilton/Noblesville

In April of 1875, the citizens of Hamilton county voted 1,205 to 724 not to replace the courthouse at Noblesville. It had been built by private subscription in 1835-1837 and many thought it was adequate, or, in any case, a new one was too expensive. The old courthouse had been built at the expense of willing individuals, such as William Conner and Josiah Polk, who donated labor or money to ensure the location of the county seat at Noblesville and the construction of a brick courthouse on the public square. But the new one could not be built that way. It would have to be built by borrowing money and taxing property owners.

So, the voters said "no."

And the commissioners built it anyway.

By the spring of 1877, any serious opposition had withered, and the county asked Edwin May to design a building for completion by 1879. May, who later would be remembered as the architect of the Indiana State House (1880-1888) at Indianapolis, had already built courthouses at Greensburg in Decatur County (1854-1860) and at Vincennes in Knox County (1872-1875). For Noblesville, he proposed a Second Empire style building with a mansard roof and a tall, square, center tower.

But once the building was under construction, the commissioners became unhappy with the way May managed the project and decided to replace him with another architect to superintend construction, J.C. Johnson of Fremont, Ohio. May sued but agreed to settle for $1,200.

The project proceeded under Johnson, who submitted plans to heat the courthouse by steam. That was practical and progressive, but not something every county in the 1870s could do. It added more than $7,000 to the tab and required the expertise of a New York City firm. The commissioners decided to eliminate some of the "needless ornament," eight statuary figures, to help pay for pipes and the boiler required for the heating system.

The Hamilton County Courthouse is a place for law and justice and ice cream and children.

Courthouse built	1877-1879
Architect	Edwin May (1824-1880), Indianapolis
Construction	Aaron G. Campfield, Winchester
Cost	$107,043
Population 1990	108,936

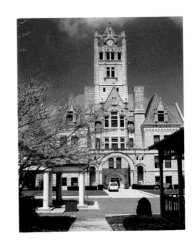

Hancock/Greenfield

The Romanesque style in Europe evolved into the Gothic, but in the United States, Gothic styles were too closely tied to church and college architecture to become a dominate style for courthouses. And yet, there are elements of the Gothic that emerge in Romanesque courthouses in Indiana, and a good example is Wing & Mahurin's design in Hancock County.

Wing & Mahurin actually built two Romanesque courthouses at the same time -- one in Greenfield and one in Starke County at Knox. Although the Starke County Courthouse was nearly $125,000 less expensive to build, the two are clearly sisters. Both have hip-roofed, Greek cross plans, steep gables and imposing central towers with steep, gabled dormers.

While the commissioners were talking about a new courthouse in 1893, a poet named James Whitcomb Riley was in town seeing about buying his family's old homestead on West Main street. His father, Reuben, had sold the home after Mrs. Riley died in 1870. Jim Riley had grown up in the eight-room house and thought it would be nice to have it back in the family.

It was because Greenfield was a county seat that the Rileys had moved there in the first place. Reuben was a lawyer in 1844 and at 26 was the youngest member of the state legislature. His poet son was born five years later and was named for Indiana's governor, James Whitcomb (1843-1848).

James lionized small-town life, and he probably expressed the feelings of many rural Hoosiers in places like Maxwell and Eden and "Tailholt" when they saw the Wing & Mahurin courthouse being built in 1896. Riley wrote:

"You kin boast about yer cities, and their stiddy growth and size
And brag about yer County-seats, and business enterprise,
And railroad, and factories, and all sich foolery--
But the little Town o' Tailholt is big enough for me!"

U.S. 40 reaches through Greenfield to the distant Indianapolis skyline.

Courthouse built	1896-1897
Architect	*Wing & Mahurin, Fort Wayne*
Construction	*Geake, Henry & Greene, Fort Wayne*
Cost	$250,692
Population 1990	45,527

The elegant marble stairway of the Hancock County Courthouse.

The first Indiana State Capitol is at the left with the Harrison County Courthouse in the background. The capital of the Indiana Territory was at Vincennes until 1813. It was then moved to Corydon, where the new state government was formed.

Harrison/Corydon

The Constitution for the new state of Indiana was written under the elms of Corydon in 1816. There were only about 64,000 Hoosiers then, living in the lower third of the state. Although William Henry Harrison had five years before, in 1811, broken the power of the Indian tribes at the Battle of Tippecanoe, most of Indiana north of Brownstown was still Indian territory.

But in the south, by 1811, Indiana was a country opening rapidly to United States settlement along the Ohio River. When the territorial capital moved to Corydon from Vincennes in 1813, territorial officials shared quarters with Harrison County officials in a small, log building, already inadequate.

By 1816, a new, stone building had been constructed and from 1816 to 1824 the Harrison County Courthouse became the Indiana State Capitol. It was the only public building in Corydon, and so not only was it used by government but also as a meeting place for political, religious and social groups.

In 1826, pressed for additional space, the Corydon Pisgah Lodge of Masons shared the cost of building a second structure to house the county clerk's office and the Masons' meeting rooms. In 1848, pressed for still more space, the county built a federal style, brick, office building east of the courthouse. Shortly thereafter, the Masons moved their meetings to the Senate Chamber of the courthouse, retaining an owner's interest in the Clerk's office until 1879.

By 1882, the county office building and the clerk's office building were razed and replaced by a new office building overshadowing the 1816 courthouse. Then in the 1920s, that office building was razed to make way for a new, grander, county courthouse. The State of Indiana acquired the old 1816 courthouse and grounds for $50,000 and restored it as the First State Capitol.

The 1928 courthouse was built in an academic style, sometimes described as classical revival.

The Harrison County Courtroom.

Courthouse built	1927-1928
Architect	*Fowler & Karges, Evansville*
Construction	*J. Fred Beggs & Co., Scottsburg*
Cost	$250,000
Population 1990	29,890

Hendricks/Danville

Builders generally took great care with the external details of Indiana's courthouses, but internal details were sometimes neglected. However, at Danville in Hendricks County, so much effort was put into internal design and decoration that use of the structure was put a year behind schedule.

Architect Clarence Martindale finished the building with fine plaster, polished marble, tinted canvas, massive bronze doors and imported walnut furniture for the courtroom. The circular rotunda, with its paired columns and sweeping stairways was a triumph of mosaic and marble and stained glass. It precedes by two years a similar rotunda by Elmer Dunlap at Delphi, 50 miles away in Carroll County (1916-1917).

Depending on what all is counted, the cost of Martindale's courthouse was between $187,000 and $225,000.

He designed an exterior of stone in the classical renaissance style that proved to be very popular during the first three decades of the century. There are a number of other pre-World War I examples, including J.W. Gaddis' courthouses at Brazil in Clay County (1912-1914), at Huntington in Huntington County (1904-1906) and at Greencastle in Putnam County (1903-1905), Lehman & Schmitt's at Peru in Miami County (1908-1910), Jesse Townsend Johnson's at Spencer in Owen County (1910-1911) and J.W. Royer's at Williamsport in Warren County (1907-1908). All of these architects, like Martindale, responded strongly to a renewed interest in classical architectural styling.

The marble in the Hendricks County Courthouse helped to push the real cost of this 1914 building to over a quarter-million dollars.

Courthouse built	*1912-1914*
Architect	*Clarence Martindale, Indianapolis*
Construction	*P.H. McCormack, Columbus*
Cost	*$186,400*
Population 1990	*75,717*

Ruth Adams works behind a wall of marble, brass and beveled glass in the Hendricks County Treasurer's office. The brass, which for years had been paint-
ed black, was restored in 1990. The glass is original.

Henry/New Castle

The commissioners of Henry County wanted a courthouse as fireproof as possible. They did not want to ever again watch their courthouse burn, as they did on a winter morning in 1865.

They wanted, and got, a new courthouse of brick and stone with walls two feet thick, with brick arches that would make wooden beams unnecessary, with a records room with no wood in the walls or floor or ceiling and with a door of steel. They wanted iron stairways and tile floors.

Isaac Hodgson gave them what they wanted, but with a mansard roof, a 110-foot clock tower, and frescoes on the ceiling of the court room. The mansard roof was unusual for a midwestern public building in the 1860s. It would become popular, but Hodgson's courthouse in Henry County was probably the earliest example of the style for public buildings in the Midwest, certainly in Indiana.

1865 might not have been the best time to take on large, public works projects. Prices were inflated and supplies scarce. But soldiers were coming home and were willing to work. The mood of the people was upbeat and patriotic, and they were willing to spend $120,000 on a building that wouldn't burn down easily.

And it was a good job for Hodgson. His other courthouses, at Martinsville in 1859 and Vernon in 1861, were much more modest projects. Still to come were his larger courthouses in Columbus (1871-1874) and Indianapolis (1869-1876, razed in 1960).

Hodgson was born in Belfast, Ireland, in 1826 and was later apprenticed to the Irish architect, Sir Charles Lamyard. He came to the United States in 1848 and eventually settled in Indianapolis where he was in charge of construction on the United States Arsenal. He worked as an architect and construction superintendent in Indianapolis until about 1880. He left Indiana for Minneapolis, although there is evidence that before his death in 1909 he was in Nebraska working on courthouse projects with his son.

Thomas E. Saunders made this statue of Abraham Lincoln from plywood, paper, fiberglass and glue for the annual Lincoln Day dinner.

Courthouse built	*1865-1869*
Architect	*Isaac Hodgson, Indianapolis*
Construction	*Henry County*
Cost	*$120,000*
Addition	*1905, $44,000*
Population 1990	*48,139*

(Opposite) Mike Redmon and his grandson, Jordon, sit on the open steps that lead to the second floor of the Henry County Courthouse.

The names of Howard County's war veterans are enshrined in the gleaming lobby of the Howard County Courthouse. The building is an unusual example of the Art Deco style of the 1930s.

Howard/Kokomo

Oscar F. Cook designed the Howard County courthouse in Kokomo with the Art Deco in mind. Its interior of stainless steel and marble reflects a style popularized in the 1920s as part of an optimistic and speed-conscious age, and again during the 1930s as a symbol of hope and progress.

But stainless steel in the courthouse was more than just a nod to fashion. It was also a nod to Elwood Haynes (1857-1925), who developed stainless steel in 1911. In many ways, the courthouse was a tribute to the innovation and modernism that characterized those inventors in Kokomo who gave the city a reputation for being imaginative.

It was at Kokomo that D.C. Spraker invented a pneumatic rubber tire and George Kingston invented a carburetor. It was at Kokomo that the first all-transistor car radio was developed. It was at Kokomo that Haynes produced the first successful commercially built gasoline-powered automobile in Indiana.

For nearly a decade Howard County had operated without a courthouse. The old one had been razed in 1927 because it was a fire hazard, but it was not a good time to rebuild. Economic troubles were already threatening Howard County even before the Great Depression. Farmers were beginning to suffer from low commodity prices. And the Haynes company filed for bankruptcy in 1924 and dissolved in 1925.

But the mid 1930s brought a kind of economic relief to the county. The decision in 1935 by the Crosley Radio Corporation to move into the Haynes body plant helped. The following year the newly formed Delco Radio Division of General Motors bought the Haynes building. And in 1937, the year the courthouse was completed, Chrysler Corporation came to town to take over the Davis Building unit of the Haynes Automobile Company.

In a spirit of confidence and a desire to put Kokomo again at the cutting edge, Cook drafted plans for a courthouse that would be different from any other in the state and would reflect the best of the 1930s.

The bronze doors of the Howard County Courthouse bear the likenesses of two favorite sons: Elwood Haynes and David Foster.

Courthouse built	*1936-1937*
Architect	*Oscar F. Cook*
Cost	*$468,000*
Population 1990	*80,827*

The balcony of the Huntington County Courthouse overlooks the image of an American eagle finely tiled into the rotunda floor. The circular rotunda with paired columns is a hallmark of several Indiana courthouses.

Huntington/Huntington

At the same time he was building the Putnam County Courthouse in Greencastle, J.W. Gaddis of Vincennes was designing one for Huntington. The cornerstone was dedicated in 1904, and the building completed in 1906 at a cost of about $346,000.

When the commissioners began to talk about a new courthouse in 1903, they expected it to cost about $200,000 and actually issued bonds in 1904 amounting to $260,000 to pay for it. That was a little short, but what they got was a fine variation on a classic design. The interior details include splendid examples of mosaic tile floors and colored marbles. The eagle mosaic on the rotunda floor is Italian tile. Gaddis used marble wainscoting, pairs of marble columns, and an arched dome of stained glass.

In addition to Huntington's courthouse, Gaddis built courthouses in Indiana at Greencastle (1904-1906) and Brazil (1912-1914). He also built courthouses in Illinois at Fairfield (1891) and Robinson (1895), and in Missouri at Perryville (1904).

The early morning sunlight reflects from the massive face and soaring columns of the Huntington County Courthouse.

Courthouse built	*1904–1906*
Architect	*John W. Gaddis (1856-1931), Vincennes*
Cost	*$346,773*
Population 1990	*35,427*

Jackson/Brownstown

In March of 1870 the Jackson County commissioners asked David Bolen to prepare plans for a new courthouse at Brownstown. The old, brick courthouse had been used since 1835. It was a two-story brick, sized at 48x32 feet.

Bolen designed the new courthouse as a large, brick structure with arched windows, quoined walls, a tall, wooden cupola and a mansard roof. A major addition was a steam heating plant.

With the heating system, the county spent about $45,000 on the building, not terribly expensive for the 1870s. By contrast, Bartholomew County at the same time was in the process of spending $225,000 on a courthouse at Columbus.

In 1910 the commissioners hired Elmer E. Dunlap of Indianapolis to enlarge Bolen's courthouse and authorized a $65,000 bond issue for the construction. The building was completed and available by May of the next year.

Dunlap's redesign was far more classical than Bolen's original. The entrance, with its columns and Ionic capitals, was, in fact, similar to the entrance he designed that same year for Franklin County at Brookville (1910-1912). At Brookville, as at Brownstown, he had recommended redesigning and expanding an old structure rather than razing and rebuilding.

The courthouse caught fire in 1959 when lightning struck it. There was extensive damage to the glass dome and to the clock as well as to the courtrooms and records, but murals on the second floor mezzanine, which had been added during the Depression years of the 1930s, were unharmed. Those murals, painted by Carl Reinbold of Seymour, depict scenes from the county's pioneer days.

Among the paintings is one of Fort Vallonia, the principal stockade in the county during the War of 1812. Vallonia was the county's oldest community, dating perhaps to 1810 and suggesting there may have been a French settlement in the late 1700s.

This Carl Reinbold painting in the county courthouse depicts the stockade at Vallonia in Jackson County during the War of 1812.

Courthouse redesigned	1910-1911
Architect	Elmer E. Dunlap, Indianapolis
Construction	Heizmann Brothers
Cost	$65,000
Population 1990	37,730

Watermelons and footlights line a temporary stage for performers at the Watermelon Festival in Brownstown.
At left is the Jackson County Courthouse.

Jasper/Rensselear

The courthouse at Rensselaer in Jasper County was built in the late 1890s in the popular Romanesque style with some Gothic and Victorian touches. The design emphasizes massing more than decoration. Architects like Alfred Grindle, who began the Jasper project, and Charles Weatherhogg, who finished it, admired the work of Henry Hobson Richardson and his philosophy that sound construction was not to be compromised by fragile ornamentation.

After the county's 1856 Greek Revival courthouse was razed to make room for the new building, the earth was excavated to the limestone bedrock and then limestone walls were built using blocks shipped from Bedford quarries. Rising from that rock foundation is a 140-foot clock tower at the center of the building.

The interior was designed to include electric lighting and more than $2,000 was paid for fancy fixtures with copper stems and frilly glass blossoms. Panels of stained glass were fitted into the arched transoms and more than $3,000 was spent on marble wainscoting.

Stained glass panels and marble wainscoting front the Auditor's office in the Jasper County Courthouse.

Courthouse built	*1896-1898*
Architect	*Alfred Grindle & Charles Weatherhogg, Fort Wayne*
Construction	*G.W. & J.F. Heinzmann, Noblesville*
Cost	*$141,732*
Population 1990	*24,960*

The courthouse square in Jasper County is as good a place as any for a tractor pull.
This one is part of the Little Cousin Jasper Festival, one of hundreds of summer festivals around the state.

Two sets of oak and walnut doors open to the courtroom on the third floor of the Jay County Courthouse. Most courtrooms in Indiana are on upper floors to permit storage of heavy records and files on the ground floor. One fortunate result of that practice has been the need for courthouses to have broad staircases and lobby areas to handle crowds.

Jay/Portland

In October of 1916, Indiana's Governor Samuel Ralston came to Portland to help celebrate the laying of the cornerstone for a new Jay County Courthouse. Ralston knew that 1916 wasn't the best time to build. There was a war and the price of labor and material was rising. In fact, this would be the only courthouse built during World War I and only one of a few courthouses ever built during wartime. A couple had been built during the Civil War, and there would be a few during the long Vietnam Conflict.

The architects took advantage of the availability of limestone from Bedford and the popularity of the revival of the classical styles.

Although it was wartime, the county treated the building project as though it were a monument to peace. Thousands of tons of dirt were hauled to the site to raise the lawn and frame the building. The interior railings were topped with mahogany. The walls were trimmed with oak and the commissioner's room finished in cherry. The interior was painted with scenes depicting the history of the area's pioneer settlement and the struggle of the Civil War -- particularly the battle at Shiloh, which was bitter for Indiana and still remembered in 1915. Stained glass and marble were used throughout the building, giving the structure a sense of light and color.

The law library in the Jay County Courthouse.

Courthouse built	*1915-1919*
Architect	*McLaughlin and Hulsken, Lima, Ohio*
Construction	*Dawson Construction Co., Pittsburgh, Pennsylvania*
Cost	*$350,000*
Population 1990	*21,512*

Jefferson/Madison

Fire on September 12, 1853 destroyed the Jefferson County Courthouse and prompted the county to hire architect David Dubach to design a new building with fireproof rooms attached to the most critical offices.

But within six years, on February 20, 1859, fire heavily damaged Dubach's new courthouse. Those special rooms could protect records, but they couldn't prevent fires.

Matthew Temperly, who in 1853 had been appointed to examine Dubach's plan and to superintend construction, painstakingly repaired the courthouse following to Dubach's detailed drawings.

A great fear of county government leaders in the mid-19th century was fire. And there was good reason for them to fear it. Every county commissioner either had experience with fires in public buildings or knew someone who had. A serious fire could destroy records -- property records, tax records, criminal records -- that were essential to govern.

Courthouses were especially vulnerable. Sometimes fires were the work of arsonists bent upon destroying records, as in Martinsville in 1876 and Washington in 1891, but more often fires were accidental. Courthouses were buildings with wood or coal-burning stoves in rooms that were lit with liquid-fuel lamps. They were furnished and finished with wooden furniture and wooden paneling. And there was lots of paper.

Dubach's restored courthouse at Madison is rectangular with a hip roof and triangular pediments centered at each side. A central dome has a high drum with louvers. The four clock faces project directly from the dome. Atop the dome is an octagonal lantern topped with a weather vane.

An almost identical courthouse exists in Switzerland County at Vevay. The commissioners there admired Madison's courthouse and in 1862 adopted plans provided by the Madison contractors Temperly and Woodfield.

As around the state the streets around the Jefferson County Courhouse become a farmer's market during the warm months.

Courthouse built	*1854-1855*
Architect	*David Dubach*
Construction	*David Dubach, Henry C. Kyle*
	& J.W. Hinds
Cost	*$36,168*
Population 1990	*29,797*

The Ohio River stretches from darkness into the twilight of a setting sun at Madison. Left behind is the spotlighted courthouse of Jefferson County.

Jennings/Vernon

Isaac Hodgson designed two Italianate style court-houses in Indiana, one at Martinsville (1857-1859) in Morgan County and one at Vernon in Jennings County (1857-1861).

The two were nearly identical when new, but later additions at Martinsville have made them distinct. Each has red brick walls with long, round-arched windows arranged in pairs and each is accented with contrasting, white stone quoins. Both have overhanging cornices crowning the campaniles. The square campaniles give these courthouses their distinctive Italian signature.

At Vernon, the courthouse was remodeled in the 1950s and renovated and restored in the 1980s. The exterior is much the same as it was in 1861. The original main entry doors were reconstructed on the east and west fronts. The weathervane atop the tower, missing since 1915, was reconstructed. A clock, contemplated in the 19th century but not installed, was added.

An Italianate style this pronounced was not typical of Indiana courthouses, but it was a style that provided a realistic alternative to the Greek Revival. It was economical while allowing the builder great freedom with details. For counties in the rural Midwest, it was a splendid idea -- stylish and practical at the same time.

The commissioners hoped to build for about $15,000. That may not have been realistic, but the final cost of just over $26,000 was a bargain compared to what prices for labor and material would become after the Civil War.

The Italianate tower of the Jennings County Courthouse is just visible through a restaurant window across the street.

Courthouse built	*1857-1861*
Architect	*Isaac Hodgson, Indianapolis*
Construction	*Samuel Read, Vernon*
Cost	*$26,375*
Renovation	*1985-1987, $669,542*
Population 1990	*23,661*

The walls of the Clerk's office in the Jennings County Courthouse are accented by pairs of tall windows which in the early days helped to provide natural lighting.

Johnson/Franklin

Just two weeks before Christmas 1874, fire destroyed the Johnson County Courthouse. It had been a lovely, brick building designed by Edwin May 25 years earlier. But in 1874 the commissioners weren't able to rebuild, and May, in his mid 50s and at the top of his career, wasn't available. He was working on a magnificent courthouse at Vincennes, one that would boost his fame considerably in Indiana as an architect of choice.

Four years later, in 1879, when the Johnson County Commissioners were able to authorize construction of a replacement courthouse, May was busy completing the Hamilton County Courthouse (1878-79) and working out his major design -- the Indiana State House. And a year later, May was dead.

Adolph Scherrer, a Swiss-born architect who came to the U.S. in 1792, assumed responsibility for completing May's State House in Indianapolis. And the Johnson County Commissioners turned to the popular George Bunting of Indianapolis to build a new courthouse in Franklin.

Bunting built the Johnson County Courthouse as he would a classic capitol. But he used pyramidal roofs at the corner pavilions and a central tower, making it very unlike anything May might have designed.

The building cost between $70,000 to $100,000 to build and about $2.3 million to renovate in 1983, when it was restored and an annex added to house government offices.

The unusual capital on this fluted column in the Johnson County Courthouse includes the special Hoosier touch of corn and flowers.

Courthouse built	*1879-1882*
Architect	*George W. Bunting (1829-1901)*
	Indianapolis
Construction	*Farman and Pearce, Indianapolis*
Cost	*$79,100*
Population 1990	*88,109*

The courthouse may be a symbol of government, but the ice cream soda is the symbol of brotherhood.
And sharing that brotherhood under the indifferent gaze of the Johnson County Courthouse are Shawn Anthony
Jeffers (with strawberry soda) and George W. White (with chocolate), both of Franklin.

Knox/Vincennes

Twenty years after architect Edwin May of Indianapolis designed the Decatur County Courthouse at Greensburg, he and his associate, Adolf Scherrer, designed this one for Knox County. Begun in 1872, it was completed four years later at a cost of between $275,000 and $360,000.

May and his Swiss-born, Vienna-trained associate used a central European, round-arched style in what contemporaries might have considered Lombard or Tuscan rather than French.

The courthouse has a different tower at each corner of a rectangular structure. Three of the towers resemble those of the Smithsonian Institution (1847-1853) in Washington, D.C., and are consistent with the architectural ideas of Robert Dale Owen, who championed the Gothic in his 1849 book, *Hints on Public Architecture*. The fourth tower, however, has a mansard roof. This irregularity among the towers gives the building a sense of being interestingly asymmetrical while in fact it is quite regular.

Originally the plans called for a brick building at an estimated cost of about $80,000. However, before construction began, the commissioners changed their minds and asked the architects to change the drawings and to switch from brick to limestone. The architects took advantage of the increased budget and technological advances to include an effective ventilation arrangement, capable of changing the air in the courtroom every 20 minutes, and installing a sewage system that included an innovation: a ladies' water closet. Only in the 1890s did public restrooms inside courthouses become common. They replaced outside privies situated on or near the courthouse lawn where they were conveniently available to the public. Even after indoor toilets became common and replaced outdoor privies, many Indiana courthouses continued to provide exterior entrances for public toilets.

A yellow ribbon honoring American troops who served in Operation Desert Storm slowly fades in the southern Indiana sunlight.

Courthouse built	1873-1876
Architect	Edwin May and Adolf Scherrer, Indianapolis
Construction	F.L. Farman for Joseph K. Frick
Cost	$360,000
Population 1990	39,884

The clock tower of the Knox County Courthouse.

Kosciusko/Warsaw

The Fort Wayne architect, Thomas J. Tolan, died in 1883 while his Kosciusko County Courthouse at Warsaw was under construction. Tolan was known and admired for his Second Empire courthouses at Lagrange and Rockville. His third one, at Warsaw, would be his last in Indiana.

His son, Brentwood, took over the firm after his father's death and continued to build spectacular courthouses -- at Columbia City, LaPorte, Fort Wayne and Muncie (razed in 1966) -- but styles were already changing. The Muncie courthouse in Delaware County would be the only one young Brentwood would build in the Second Empire style, with massing almost identical to that at Rockport and Warsaw. In a sense it was a final tribute to the 1870s and to his father.

But even at Warsaw there were already hints of a shift to a more classical style. Although the mansard roofs of the Second Empire are prominent, the detail is less Victorian than its nearest relative at Rockville (1879-1881), and the central tower is topped by an octagonal dome rather than a pyramid.

The entrance to the Kosciusko County Courthouse.

Courthouse built	*1882-1884*
Architect	*Thomas J. Tolan (1831-1883) and*
	Brentwood S. Tolan (1855-1923),
	Fort Wayne
Construction	*Hiram Iddings*
Cost	*$197,800*
Population 1990	*65,294*

This etched glass window in the Circuit Courtroom at Warsaw testifies to the underlying simplicity and care for detail that went into the sophisticated courthouses designed by Thomas and Brentwood Tolan.

The clock tower of the Lagrange County Courthouse.

Lagrange/Lagrange

At the cornerstone dedication for the Lagrange County Courthouse in 1878, attorney John B. Howe, a senior member of the bar, remarked that this new building was going to cost as much as the whole county was worth. The construction bid had been $46,700. Howe said a courthouse should be like justice itself, simple and without ostentation, but since it was the fashion to build expensive public buildings, he would do his part.

And because of his support and that of others, Lagrange County built a brick and sandstone courthouse with a clock tower that soars to 125 feet. The interior has fine examples of late 19th century woodwork.

The final cost of the courthouse at LaGrange came in at $25,000 over the contract price. But even at $75,675, the building was the least costly of the courthouses in Indiana designed by Thomas J. Tolan. The limestone building at Rockville, built at almost the same time (1879-81), was much more lavish and about $40,000 more expensive. The courthouse at Warsaw (1882-84) cost Kosciusko County $197,800. Thomas Tolan's son, Brentwood, built courthouses at Columbia City (1888-1890) for $148,793, La Porte (1892-1893) for $281,235 and Fort Wayne (1897-1900) for $817,554.

One way to control some construction costs was to skimp a little on plumbing and heating. At LaGrange the courthouse was built with running water but central heating was deferred. Each room was heated as needed by a stove. When properly installed and maintained, the stoves were fine, but they were a nuisance and always somewhat of a risk. The LaGrange courthouse, although it stayed temporarily with outmoded technology, was nevertheless constructed by the Tolans in a way that could allow central heating to be added later.

The heavy, wooden banister in the Lagrange County Courthouse curves gracefully up to the Circuit Courtroom.

Courthouse built	1878-1879
Architect	Thomas J. Tolan (1831-1883) and Brentwood S. Tolan (1855-1923) Fort Wayne
Construction	Charles Bosseker and John Begue, Fort Wayne
Cost	$71,675.32
Population 1990	29,477

Lake/Crown Point

The old courthouse in Lake County has been preserved as a national treasure and has been a registered national landmark since 1973. Although county business is no longer conducted in the building but rather at a large, government complex on the city's north side, it is the old building that speaks with romantic elegance of the life and style of local government.

After all, this was the place where silent film star Rudolph Valentino got his marriage license in 1923.

It was designed by Chicago architect John C. Cochrane, who also designed the Illinois state capitol, and was completed in 1879 at a cost of $52,000. The county had saved $60,000 in advance for the construction and was able to pay for the building upon completion, with money left over.

The architecture is eclectic and original. Cochrane used elements of Victorian, Romanesque and Georgian styles, but overall it has an Academic flavor. When additions were made in 1907 and 1928, Cochrane's heirs remained faithful to the original vision, reproducing the lines of Cochrane's two-story center structure.

Cochrane's only other courthouse in Indiana is at Valparaiso in neighboring Porter County (1883-1885). That courthouse was extensively rebuilt after a disastrous fire in 1934. Other examples of Cochrane courthouses from the same period can be found in Illinois, Missouri and Iowa.

In 1971, the county built the Lake County Government Complex on a 70-acre tract. The three buildings are of steel and glass and house a jail, courts and administrative offices.

The old Lake County Courthouse has been preserved but is no longer used for government business.

Courthouse built	1878-1879
Architect	John C. Cochrane (1833-1887), Chicago
Construction	Thomas and Hugh Colwell
Cost	$52,000
1906 addition	$160,000
1928 addition	$80,000
Population 1990	475,594

The Lake County Government Complex was built in 1971 on a 70-acre tract at the north edge of Crown Point.

LaPorte/LaPorte

Brentwood Tolan of Fort Wayne designed the Richardsonian Romanesque courthouse at LaPorte. The style was popular in the 1890s but was a little unusual for Brentwood or for his father, Thomas. Their Indiana courthouses were typically much more Second Empire or Beaux Arts in attitude.

Still, the LaPorte courthouse, with its red sandstone walls, demonstrated Tolan's independent mastery of the Romanesque. Above the basement, all the windows were designed with round arches and stained glass transoms. The central tower was built with large windows near its base to light the interior. The belfry's broad, open arches, although not unusual, were not inspired by Henry Hodson Richardson, whose work a decade earlier produced a Romanesque revival in public architecture and a host of imitators.

Interior detail was always important to the Tolans and is a notable feature in the Tolan courthouses. At LaPorte, Brentwood used rich paneling and gilded friezes. He used beveled plate glass and leaded patterns of stained glass in doors and windows.

This remarkable structure was LaPorte's third courthouse and the first paid for from tax funds. In the earlier years of the 19th century it was common for courthouses to be built with private money or by the sale of public land. But as prices moved well into the six figures, the typical way to support an ambitious building project was by tax levy. Only in a few cases did counties create a sinking fund for future construction. Most often they borrowed the money.

Indiana law was unusually liberal when it came to taxes. It allowed commissioners to appropriate any funds in the county treasury, to borrow up to one per cent of all appraised real and personal property without an election and to levy and collect whatever taxes were necessary to build a courthouse whenever the commissioners thought such a building was necessary. Taxpayers could protest at a public hearing, but they were invariably overruled.

LaPorte County's courthouse rises above Howard A. Demyer's sculpture of a Potawatomi Indian with broken spear, symbolizing peace.

Courthouse built	1892-1894
Architect	Brentwood S. Tolan (1855-1923),
	Fort Wayne
Construction	Charles A. Moses, Chicago
Cost	$328,000
Population 1990	107,066

Circuit Court Judge Robert Gettinger sits behind the bench in the LaPorte County Courthouse. His courtroom is graced with original stained glass windows and carved woodwork.

Seated at the bench in the courtroom of the Lawrence County Courthouse is Judge Linda Chezem. Judge Chezem was the first woman appointed, later elected, to a circuit court judgeship in Indiana. She was also the first County Court judge in the state. Today she sits on the Court of Appeals of Indiana.

Lawrence/Bedford

When the Lawrence County Commissioners hired architect Walter Scholar to design a courthouse in Bedford, they asked him to preserve the north wall of the old, limestone courthouse. Scholar did, not only keeping the old wall but letting the 1870 building determine much of what he did with the new structure. His final design was a classical renaissance style building -- simple, elegant, dignified -- that could show off the beauty and the durability of the native stone.

It is said the reason for replacing the 1870 building in 1930 was that Lawrence County's ardent basketball fans -- who enjoyed celebrating on the courthouse square -- were a threat to the fragile, old building. The real reason was that the old building was much too small and, with its wooden roof and floors, much too susceptible to fire.

Courthouses, such as Bedford's, were not only office buildings but also archives. Paper records of all kinds were stored permanently in the buildings -- property transactions, mortgages, assessments, deeds, marriage records, court records, military records. All of these files were at risk in a building with too much old wood and old wiring.

The ideal building for storing records was one as fireproof as possible, one with stone walls and floors, iron beams in the superstructure, and plaster and concrete interior walls. In most Indiana courthouses, wood floors -- like fireplaces and wood stoves -- were abandoned whenever there was an opportunity to rebuild. Bedford was one of four major courthouse construction projects between 1925 and 1930 motivated by security concerns and space needs. Hoosiers built new courthouses at Sullivan in 1926, at Corydon in 1929 and, after a disastrous fire, at Washington in 1929. Both Sullivan and Washington, like Bedford, used Indiana limestone while Corydon used limestone and brick.

Don Buck, who came to watch a trial in the Lawrence County Courthouse, pauses in the courthouse stairwell.

Courthouse built	*1930*
Architect	*Walter Scholar*
Cost	*$390,000*
Population 1990	*42,836*

The glass exterior of the Madison County's 1973 courthouse reflects the color and texture of its surroundings in Anderson.

Madison/Anderson

In the early 1970s Madison County replaced its 19th century brick courthouse with a much larger structure of glass, steel and brick. County officials had argued for a new building for 25 years before they successfully displaced the old, 20,000-square-foot courthouse with a new one containing the much-needed 95,000 square feet.

Some counties, such as Floyd in 1961, Marion in 1962, Delaware in 1969, Clark in 1970, White in 1976 and Cass in 1979, have replaced aging courthouses, and a few, such as Vanderburgh and Lake, have preserved the old buildings while no longer using them for county government. Still, more than half of the Indiana courthouses housing local governmental offices today were built in the 19th century.

The 1973 building replaced one built in 1882-1885 designed by George W. Bunting of Indianapolis. Bunting was a popular courthouse architect, and examples of his work can be found at Bloomfield, Liberty, Bluffton, Crawfordsville, Frankfort and Franklin. He also built the courthouse at Washington, lost to fire in 1927. Bunting probably designed more courthouses in Indiana than any other architect, including his popular Fort Wayne competitor, T.J. Tolan and Son.

Although there were construction problems with the 1973 building that led to expensive renovation and additions, the building is a good example of a late 20th century courthouse that, even with its striking lack of ornamentation, has continued to cling to traditional symbols of clocks and towers. Instead of porticoes and public lawns, Johnson and Ritchhart designed a public plaza, much of it protected by cover. The plaza contains a podium, garden walls, a fountain, trees and a display of relics from the old courthouses that preceded it.

Andy Conover, drainage coordinator for Madison County, works at his drawing table inside the courthouse.

Courthouse built	*1972-1973*
Architect	*Johnson, Ritchhart & Associates*
Cost	*$4 million*
Reconstruction	*1983, $1.7 million*
Population 1990	*130,669*

Marion/Indianapolis

In 1962 Marion County replaced an ornate, 19th century courthouse with a 28-story office building of glass and steel. The old courthouse, originally built in 1877, had three towers along a mansard roofline. The center tower was a domed, clock tower and a sometime vantage point for a fire watch over the city.

The old courthouse, while a magnificent example of 19th century courthouse architecture was woefully inadequate by the middle of the 20th century. Its detractors described it as a begrimed, old relic of the Victorian Era. The move to replace it began in the 1940s, and in 1953 the state of Indiana gave Marion County clear title to the courthouse site, amounting to an entire city block bounded by Delaware, Market, Alabama and Washington streets. In the same year, Indianapolis and Marion County created a City-County Building Authority to oversee the construction of a massive office complex.

In 1957 the Authority and the architects agreed on a design to accent utility and practicality: A tall tower with flanking wings to house the courts and police.

Ground breaking came on an unseasonably cold October 30, 1959. About 80 officials and civic leaders took turns trying to dig into the earth of the old courthouse parking lot with chromium-plated shovels.

And by January 2, 1962, the first county employees moved into the building from the old courthouse. Throughout the spring and summer employees moved their offices, including judges and the staffs of 15 different courts. Meanwhile, city offices from the old Indianapolis city hall and from other buildings leased by the city were moved into the new building. By the end of the 1960s, the building, with a million square feet of floor space, housed 2,250 local government workers.

The City-County Building for Indianapolis and Marion County overshadows the old city market area in downtown Indianapolis.

Courthouse built	*1960-1962*
Architect	*Allied Architects & Engineers, Indianapolis*
Construction	*Huber, Hunt & Nichols, Inc.*
Cost	*$25.5 million*
Population 1990	*797,159*

Fourth of July fireworks burst over the City-County Building in Indianapolis.
This 28 story office complex was completed in 1962.

Marshall/Plymouth

The Marshall County Courthouse is a Gordon P. Randall design built in the early 1870s. Randall, a Chicago architect, published a series of illustrated publications in the 1860s to promote his work. In his publications he made suggestions to commissioners and offered to reward readers who provided information leading to commissions.

He was eager to design courthouses and submitted proposals to Wabash, Parke, Benton and Marshall counties in Indiana. He got the jobs at Benton and Marshall, plus two more in Illinois and one in Michigan.

For the Marshall County Courthouse at Plymouth, Randall designed an impressive clock tower over a brick and stone building with Corinthian porticoes. The vermiculated quoins at the corners and the ornamental hoods at the windows were concessions to the Victorian.

Those vermiculated quoins -- with their twisting patterns cut into the stone -- were a bit unusual in Indiana but not unique. J.C. Johnson used them in Decatur at about the same time on the Adams County Courthouse (1872-1873).

A stained-glass transom arches over Melita Thompson's door in the bailiff's office in Marshall County.

Courthouse built	*1870-1872*
Architect	*Gordon P. Randall, Chicago*
Construction	*Epperson& Favorite, Lafayette*
Cost	*$109,254*
Population 1990	*42,182*

*The newly designed and built Marshall County Courts building
is in the foreground, right, of the courthouse built in the 1870s*

The Martin County Courthouse at Shoals.

Martin/Shoals

Hoosiers usually moved their county seats once or twice during the 19th century, but Martin County holds the record. The seat moved repeatedly before settling in Shoals after the Civil War.

On January 24, 1828, the Indiana General Assembly approved the evacuation of the county seat from Hindostan to Mt. Pleasant. There wasn't much to move. Most of the population had already left or died from disease. Sickness had swept through the town, leaving hardly enough healthy mourners to bury their dead.

The move to Mt. Pleasant, overlooking the east fork of the White River, was completed by March, and a courthouse was hastily constructed. Then from Mt. Pleasant the seat moved to the more centrally situated Halberts Bluffs in 1844 and to Hillsborough (Dover Hill) in 1845.

Harrisonville, Loogootee and Memphis (Shoals) all competed for the seat, but by 1869 a compromise placed it at a new town, to be platted as West Shoals on the opposite side of the river from Memphis (Shoals).

A brick courthouse was built there in 1871 for about $29,000. That building burned in 1876 -- one of several major courthouse fires during the 1870s -- but the commissioners were able save the records, and they were able to rebuild a simple, brick two-story building on the same foundation.

The building has 18-feet high ceilings, an iron-railed balcony and an unusual circular stairway.

*Evelyn Earl and Bill Strange talk
in the Martin County Treasurer's office.*

Courthouse built	1876-1877
Architect	William P. George
Construction	Travis & Benjamin Carter
Cost	$8,588
Population 1990	10,369

Miami/Peru

In the fall of 1905 the county commissioners of Miami County, John G. Davis, James S. Blair and Alfred Ramsey, appropriated $280,000 of borrowed money for a new courthouse. They chose Theodore Schmitt of Cleveland, Ohio, to be the architect.

That was not a happy decision for Clarkson W. Macy, the county auditor, and he filed a lawsuit seeking to stop construction. Litigation proceeded for two years and ended only after the Indiana Supreme Court ruled that the Miami County commissioners had the power to let contracts and hire architects.

Macy lost in court, but the commissioners lost at the polls. None of the incumbents at the next election were re-elected to office. The marble plaque inside the west entrance lists the names of six commissioners: the three who selected the architect, Davis, Blair and Ramsey, and the three who were in office in 1910, Thomas M. Busby, Timothy M. Ginney and Charles J. Ward. Two other commissioners, Jacob Casper and James W. Hurst, who served three-year terms during the construction, are not listed. The plaque also lists two auditors who served during the period: Charles Griswold and Frank K. McElheny. Macy, who was auditor when the contracts were let but who opposed the construction, is not included.

Construction of the Indiana limestone building began in 1908 and was completed just before the end of 1910. Schmitt designed a building in the classical renaissance style that became immensely popular after the World's Columbian Exposition in Chicago in 1893. The exposition promoted what was thought to be the best of classical and renaissance design, and it helped to make Indiana limestone a favorite material for large, public buildings.

During the period after the turn of the century, similar buildings of limestone were built in Spencer (1910-1911), Brazil (1912-1914), Greencastle (1903-1905), Auburn (1911-1914), Bloomington (1907-1908), Danville (1912-1914) and Huntington (1904-1906).

This "Doughboy" statue honors the Miami County soldiers and sailors who served in World War I.

Courthouse built	*1908-1910*
Architect	*Lehman & Schmitt, Cleveland*
Construction	*P.H. McCormack & Co., Columbus*
Cost	*$251,000*
Population 1990	*36,897*

A witness testifies in Judge Bruce Embrey's courtroom in the Miami County Courthouse.

Monroe/Bloomington

The Monroe County Courthouse was completed in 1908. A year earlier, Judge Wilson, watching the placement of the cornerstone, said this building showed the world that Monroe County believes in government and in law. And in true southern Indiana fashion, he found a moral for life in the construction of such a building. The lesson, he said, is to always "be square, plumb and level."

Square and plumb it is. The building is in a classical renaissance style associated with the Ecole des Beaux Arts in Paris. Although few Indiana architects were trained in France, the Beaux Arts classicism had a tremendous impact on Indiana courthouse design. Paul Goeldner notes in his research on midwestern courthouses that the beginning of the 20th century was a time before which courthouses in the Beaux Arts tradition were rare and after which "they were rarely anything else." Indiana, Goeldner notes, was especially receptive to this Beaux Arts style because it helped to popularize Indiana's limestone.

The popularity of 19th century designs, such as Orange County's Greek Revival courthouse in Paoli or Martin County's Italianate courthouse in Martinsville or Starke county's Romanesques courthouse in Knox, were largely swept away with the impact of the World's Columbian Exposition in Chicago in 1892. The Exposition introduced a fine-arts fashion that claimed to reach for what was then understood to be the best in classical design.

The 1908 courthouse in Bloomington replaced a graceful brick building constructed originally in 1826 under the direction of John Ketcham. That building was expanded and remodeled in the 1850s and again in the 1870s. When it was replaced in 1908, its unusual weather vane was saved and mounted at the top of the new courthouse dome. It is a 45-inch, or, depending who you believe, a 66-inch copper fish.

In 1984 the courthouse was extensively renovated at a cost of $2.3 million.

Bill Dahman carved Bloomington's Peace Statue in 1979. The dove in her hand was lost in the '80s and remade in 1991 by Bill Galloway.

Courthouse built	*1907-1908*
Architect	*Wing & Mahurin, Fort Wayne*
Construction	*Drake & Caldwell*
Cost	*$188,000*
Population 1990	*108,978*

The Monroe County Courthouse is strung with thousands of lights during the Christmas Holiday season.

Montgomery/Crawfordsville

The Montgomery County Courthouse in Crawfordsville was George Bunting's first in Indiana. Today there are six Bunting courthouse still standing in the state, and his buildings can be found in Michigan, Illinois, Ohio, Tennessee, West Virginia and Kansas.

Bunting graduated from Girard College and joined the Confederacy during the Civil War, serving as a colonel in the First Mississippi Cavalry. In 1869, he moved north and by 1874 was in Indianapolis with the firm of Bunting and Huebner, and later, by the mid 1880s, with Bunting and Son.

Although the Montgomery County Courthouse has the distinction of being designed by a former Confederate officer, it was a former Union officer who spoke at the dedication of the cornerstone in 1875. Gen. Lew Wallace, a Civil War hero, author of the best-selling book, *Ben Hur*, and Crawfordsville lawyer, spoke of the life of the court. Wallace wanted it to be remembered that courthouses were public buildings and had been used in pragmatic ways.

"How the ancient auditorium has rung with the cheers of excited factions! What partisan debates the two great pillars of this room have witnessed! It has been the scene of inquest of coroners and of post-mortem examinations by doctors. On the other hand its walls have been hung with garlands for the festival and countless times echoed to the music of minstrels, lecturers and preachers. Congregations too poor to own churches and despised sects and professors of new and unpopular isms have always found here a pulpit and freedom of speech if not vast audiences. And hither the Godless gambler has stolen, hard upon the dismissal of the Sunday school. In and about it the recruiting drums of two great wars have roared like the sea."

The Montgomery County memorial to its military veterans who died during World War II.

Courthouse built	1875-1876
Architect	George W. Bunting (1829-1901), Indianapolis
Construction	McCormack & Sweeney, Columbus
Cost	$150,000
Population 1990	34,436

When the Montgomery County Courthouse was renovated in the 1980s
the massive wood doors to the first floor offices were preserved and refinished.

Morgan/Martinsville

Indiana does not have many Italianate style courthouses, but Isaac Hodgson designed two: one at Martinsville (1857-1859) in Morgan County and one at Vernon in Jennings County (1857-1861).

When new, the two were nearly identical, but additions at Martinsville have made them distinct. Each has red brick walls with long, round-arched windows arranged in pairs, and each is accented with contrasting, white, stone quoins. Both have overhanging modillion cornices crowning the campaniles. It is really the square campaniles that give these courthouses their distinctive Italian signature.

The major changes at Martinsville came in 1977 when a new east wing was added and the old section remodeled and restored. At that time the circuit courtroom, which had been modified over the years, was restored to its original design and a clock was installed in the campanile.

Morgan County's Italianate style was an alternative to the ever popular Greek Revival. It allowed more flexibility and greater freedom with details, but it was not a typical architecture for courthouses, and most examples are concentrated in rural Missouri, Illinois and Indiana where there was a desire for stylish practicality. The design had the great advantage of being stylish and reasonably priced.

Fire damaged the courthouse in 1876 and records in the offices of the county auditor and clerk were burned. The fire was thought to be arson, perhaps by an official trying to conceal evidence. In any case, the danger of fire was such a threat in the mid-19th century that it became one of the most often cited reasons for courthouse replacement in the post-Civil War era. As a result, Indiana has only a few pre-war courthouses still standing. There are those in Morgan (1857-1859), Jennings (1857-1861), Decatur (1854-1860), Jefferson (1854-1855) and St. Joseph (1853-1855) counties and a few older ones in Harrison County (1814-1816), in Ohio County (1844-1844) and in Orange County (1847-1850).

The judge's bench in the Morgan County Courthouse.

Courthouse built	1857-1859
Architect	Isaac Hodgson (1826-1909)
Construction	Perry M. Blankenship, Martinsville
Cost	$32,000
Renovation	1974-1976, $1,347,343
Population 1990	55,920

Morgan County Courthouse on an autumn afternoon.

Newton/Kentland

That the county courthouse would be or should be in Kentland was, in the beginning, a matter of debate. The location of county seats in Indiana was of great commercial interest to local businesses during the 1800s. It was widely believed, and rightly, that the location of county government provided an important commercial advantage for a city.

Generally, county seats were located near the center of counties so that it would never be farther away than a day's ride by wagon from any part of the county. Kentland was an exception. It was at the extreme southern edge of Newton County, and so was vulnerable to efforts by at Brook, Morocco, Beaver City and Goodland to have it moved.

They tried, repeatedly. Beaver City even built its own courthouse as an inducement. In 1899, a new state statute provided for relocation of county seats by election, and Morocco, Brook and Goodland all tried again to wrest the seat from Kentland.

Actually, Goodland won the election with a vote of 1,834 for the move and 697 against, but it lost an ensuing court battle when the Indiana Supreme Court found the 1899 statute unconstitutional. It was a victory for Kentland, but six years later the commissioners were back in court fighting an effort to prevent them from replacing the 1861 courthouse in Kentland.

In the spring of 1905, the commissioners had contracted for the construction of a courthouse to be built in a simple, but academic, style. It would replace a 45-year-old building that was too small and too frail. The opposition sued to stop construction and won, arguing that the county had failed to appropriate funds by ordinance. But it was a weak victory, one based only on a too easily corrected technicality. Once out of court, the commissioners appropriated by ordinance and the courthouse went up.

The new buff brick and limestone building would cost about $35,000. Still, that was modest for 1906. Huntington County built one that same year for $350,000.

About 60 years ago Herman Dieclam painted this metal door to look like wood with a fine finish.

Courthouse built	1905-1906
Architect	*Joseph T. Hutton, Hammond*
Construction	*Eric Lund, Hammond*
Cost	$35,000
Population 1990	13,551

(opposite) Most Indiana county seats are located near the center of a county, an exception is Kentland in southern Newton County.

Natural history exhibits are a permanent part of several Indiana courthouses. This one in the Noble County Courthouse basement presents animals that are native to the Ablion area.

Noble/Albion

The Noble County Courthouse in Albion is a brick, Romanesque building designed by E.O. Fallis, a Toledo, Ohio architect originally from Lagro, Indiana. This was Fallis' only Indiana courthouse, although he built others in Illinois, Michigan and Ohio.

Fallis' design, while Romanesque, was not strongly influenced by the premier Romanesque architect of the 1880s, Boston's Henry Hobson Richardson. It was lighter, more asymmetrical than the work typical of Richardson, and it was built before Richardson's influence penetrated deeply into Indiana fashion of the 1890s.

Communities like Albion emerged in northern Indiana in the 1830s and saw their future growth dependent on becoming a county seat. Without that status there was every chance of being doomed to the backwoods prosperity of abundant game and little cash. But being a county seat attracted bankers, retailers and professionals. Albion was one of several Noble County communities that fought for recognition as the county seat in the 1840s. Between 1836 and 1844, the prize moved to three different sites -- first to Sparta, than to Augusta in 1837 and finally to Port Mitchell in 1844. Ligonier, Lisbon, Center (later called Albion) and Wolf Lake all tried to wrest it from Port Mitchell. And in 1846, the site finally settled on Center after a run-off election with Augusta and the incumbent Port Mitchell.

Nineteenth century planners always hoped to locate county seats in the geographic center of a county. In Indiana that meant placing the seat roughly a day's wagon ride more or less from any part of the county. Politics and topography could interfere with that goal and often did but not in Noble County.

Albion had the central location and the good sense to keep the name Center until the move was made.

A couple chat in the Noble County Courthouse rotunda near a photograph of former Secretary of Agriculture Earl Butz.

Courthouse built	*1887-1889*
Architect	*E.O. Fallis & Co. (1851 -1927)*
Cost	*$101,604*
Population 1990	*37,877*

Ohio/Rising Sun

The oldest courthouse in Indiana that has been continuously used is the Greek Revival building at Rising Sun in Ohio County. It is a simple, Doric design. Available records fail to tell how much it cost or who the designer was, but Pinkney and John James, who laid out Rising Sun, probably were influential in determining the style.

It would not have been difficult for the builders to find a Greek Revival design in the 1840s. Pattern books were widely available and widely used, and although they didn't provide plans, they did provide details.

It is probably because pattern books didn't provide plans that none of the surviving Greek Revival courthouses are identical. Builders had a good deal of freedom to adapt to local needs and tastes, and the basic design of the Greek Revival was simple enough that they didn't need complicated technology -- such as steam hoists -- or knowledge of sophisticated construction techniques to do the job.

There are only two other examples of Greek Revival courthouses from this period in Indiana. The Orange County Courthouse in Paoli (1847-1859) was built just three years after the one at Rising Sun and is a good example of the Doric style. The 1853-1855 courthouse at South Bend is also essentially Greek Revival, but its architect, John Mills Van Osdel, was a Chicago professional who departed widely from the pattern books.

A memorial to the men and women of Ohio County who have served in the armed forces.

Courthouse built	*1844*
Population 1990	*5,315*

The Ohio County Courthouse, the oldest courthouse continuously used in Indiana.

Orange/Paoli

The two oldest Indiana courthouses that have been used continuously are in Orange County (1847-1850) and Ohio County (1844). Both are Greek Revival designs, a style dominate in the pre-Civil War era. Pattern books helped to make the style popular. It also helped that construction could be relatively simple and that the classic origin of the design was strongly appealing as a symbol of democracy.

Paoli is an excellent example of the type. It has a Doric portico with six fluted columns constructed of brick with a cement surface and stone caps. The stairs are made of ornamental iron and the square cupola is topped by a bell-shaped roof. It is simple, elegant and symbolic.

Courthouses built in the 19th and early 20th centuries had social as well as governmental functions and were built on wide lawns that not only emphasized the building but also served as a public park, as a place where preachers, pedlars and politicians could preach, pedal and politic.

Samuel Ralston remembered the Orange County courthouse in 1912 when he stood on the lawn campaigning as the Democratic gubernatorial candidate. The audience was not sympathetic and the editor of the Paoli *Republican* remarked that Ralston's speech was fairly good "for a man who was on the wrong side." Ralston that fall became Indiana's 28th governor.

And there are other memories from Paoli that describe life at courthouses all over the state. There was the August afternoon in 1912 when Tri Kappa raised $85 by selling ice cream, sherbets and popcorn balls on the lawn. There was a day in 1877 when Dr. Gifford came from Kokomo to lecture about the medicinal value of cold water. There were the days when the clock tower bell rang to announce a session of court and rang again when the verdict was returned. And there was the day in 1970 when fire damaged part of the clock tower and put the clock out of commission for nearly a month.

The fluted columns of the Orange County Courthouse.

Courthouse built	*1847-1850*
Construction	*Orange County*
Cost	*$14,000*
Population 1990	*18,409*

A tradition around courthouses, somewhat less honored today, has been to gather to gab and gossip on the courthouse lawn, as these men are apparently doing in Paoli.

The courthouse square is the place to be footloose in sweet Owen County. More people gather around courthouses for the good times than for any other reason. More people are involved in festivals -- such as the Owen County's Apple Butter Festival -- than are ever involved in the details of local government.

Owen/Spencer

In 1883 James W. Archer of Owen County thought this whole business of building fancy courthouses was silly. Archer had been a farmer and a storekeeper and a prospector, and he thought the 1824 courthouse in Spencer was just fine. It was brick and solid and in good repair. It even had been enlarged and remodeled a couple of times.

"We are not in a hurry, as some other counties have been, to build a gorgeous courthouse, with a mortgage on top of it," he wrote.

"If the generations succeeding us need a larger and finer courthouse, let them build it when the county grows populous enough to require it."

And that is exactly what later generations did.

In 1910, the commissioners hired Jesse Townsend Johnson to design an Owen County Courthouse in native limestone using the classical renaissance style that was becoming so popular. They were ready for a larger and finer courthouse.

Similar buildings had already been built at Greencastle in Putnam County (1903-1905), at Peru in Miami County (1908-1910), at Huntington in Huntington County (1904-1906) and at Williamsport in Warren County (1907-1908). They all were marked by their attention to detail, their fine stone work and their adherence to an ideal vision of a system of justice symbolized in the order and power of classical Greek and Roman styling.

Johnson was a serious architect and widely known for his schools, lodges and churches. After the Owen County project and World War I, he went to Washington to help redesign Arlington National cemetery, which design would include a tomb dedicated to the Unknown Soldier. Johnson, too, would eventually be buried at Arlington.

A memorial to the Owen County men and women who served in World War I.

Courthouse built	*1910-1911*
Architect	*Jesse Townsend Johnson*
Cost	*$106,000*
Population 1990	*17,281*

Every year thousands of people go to Rockville to eat chicken. Actually Rockville is the jumping off place for exploring Parke County's historic covered bridges. Chicken is what you get at the courthouse whether you find bridges or not.

Parke/Rockville

Depending on how you count it, the Parke County Courthouse by Thomas J. Tolan and his son, Brentwood, cost either $79,000 or $111,000 in the early 1880s. The higher figure reflects the cost of a new jail, which was part of the same project and bond issue. But however the money is counted, the courthouse project at Rockville was a major work for the Tolans, one that established their reputation and one that strongly influenced subsequent designs at Warsaw and Muncie.

Three Tolan courthouses were under construction simultaneously in 1880: this one at Rockville, one at Lagrange (1878-1879) and a third in Cambridge, Illinois (1878-1880). The Tolans would eventually design seven courthouses in Indiana, six of which still stand, as well as courthouses in Ohio, Iowa, Illinois and Tennessee. The Tolans would use a variety of styles in Indiana, including the Second Empire as in Rockville, the Romanesque as in LaPorte (1892-1893) and the Beaux Arts as in Fort Wayne (1897-1900), the latter two by Brentwood after his father's death in 1883.

Other Tolan courthouses in Indiana include those in Warsaw in Kosciusko County (1882-1884), Columbia City in Whitley County (1888-1890) and Muncie in Delaware County (1885-1887, razed in 1966).

Only George Bunting of Indianapolis was the architect for more Indiana courthouses, but not even Bunting produced the range of style and imagination that came from Thomas and Brentwood Tolan, whose courthouses represent a continuous transition in taste from the 1870s to 1900.

The Parke County Circuit Courtroom.

Courthouse built	*1879-1882*
Architect	*Thomas J. Tolan (1831-1883) and*
	Brentwood S. Tolan (1855-1923),
	Fort Wayne
Construction	*W.H. Myers, Fort Wayne*
Cost	*$111,156*
Population 1990	*15,410*

Perry/Cannelton

The Perry County Courthouse was designed by Louisville architect John Bacon Hutchins and completed in 1897. Unlike the massive, Richardsonian Romanesque style so popular in Indiana in the 1890s, Hutchins used a more classical style with straw-colored, pressed brick and cut trimmings of Bedford limestone.

Cannelton is an Ohio River town, and there was a time before the Civil War when one could watch the river and see a steamboat moving toward or away from the port of Louisville at any time of the day or night.

In 1859 the Perry County seat was moved from Rome to Cannelton and the commissioners used a remodeled school for the courthouse. However, Cannelton had a competitor, another river town called Tell City. Citizens there also wanted the seat for Perry County, and although neither was centrally located, both were almost the only places with the population and the prosperity to pay for the privilege.

Operating from the premise that the city with the courthouse would get the seat, each raised money by public subscription and each built a courthouse in the 1890s. The trophy went to Cannelton, and the Tell City citizens settled for one of the state's more interesting city halls.

However, Tell City never gave up. In 1991 the Perry County commissioners voted to relocate to Tell City and to build a $2.6 million government center.

If the county seat moves again, it will be Perry County's fourth: Troy from 1815 to 1818, Rome from 1818 to 1859 and Cannelton from 1859.

This City Hall building in Tell City was once in contention to become the Perry County Courthouse.

Courthouse built	*1896-1897*
Architect	*John Bacon Hutchins, Louisville*
Construction	*Charles Hafel & Sons, Cannelton*
Cost	*$30,000*
Population 1990	*19,107*

*Connie Berger works on the Assessor's books in the Perry County Courthouse
in Cannelton, about four miles upriver from Tell City.*

Kern Luker changes a lightbulb in the rotunda of the Pike County Courthouse.

Pike/Petersburg

Elmer Dunlap's firm in Indianapolis was working on two courthouses in 1921 -- one at Petersburg in Pike County and another at Rockport in Spencer County.

The prototype for both of these was his courthouse at Delphi in Carroll County, built in 1916-1917. All three used circular rotundas with stained glass ceilings. All three were designed in an almost understated classic style. The big differences are embellishment. Delphi was his most elaborate and Petersburg his simplest.

Dunlap did not use Delphi's interior columns at Petersburg, but he did keep the flat arches, the graceful sweep of railings and the sense of open space.

This was Pike County's fourth courthouse. The first was a log structure built in 1818. That was replaced in 1836 and again in 1868 by brick buildings.

The 1922 courthouse was one of only six built in Indiana during the 1920s. All were built in a similar classical style, although by a variety of architects. These, along with Lawrence County's 1930 courthouse in Bedford, would prove to be the last of the classical courthouses in Indiana. Besides Rockport and Petersburg, courthouses related in exterior design were built during this decade at Sullivan in Sullivan County (1926), Corydon in Harrison County (1927-1929), Newport in Vermillion County (1923-1925) and Washington in Daviess County (1928-1929).

Pike County women gather to quilt at the Petersburg Senior Citizens' Center in the courthouse basement.

Courthouse built	*1920-1922*
Architect	*Elmer E. Dunlap, Indianapolis*
Construction	*Jasper N. Good, Columbus*
Cost	*$252,031*
Population 1990	*12,509*

Porter/Valparaiso

Valparaiso's daily newspaper, The *Vidette-Messenger*, published an extra edition two days after Christmas in 1934 announcing the loss of the county courthouse.

COURT HOUSE DESTROYED BY FIRE
Loss Estimated at Half Million
4 LAPROTE FIREMAN INJURED

The fire during the early morning of December 27 lit the downtown area. Local restaurants opened to a depression-era crowd who sat through the night watching an expensive 1885 building struggle in the sub-zero weather. The courthouse had been designed by John C. Cochrane, who, among other projects, designed the Lake County Courthouse in Crown Point and the Illinois State Capitol.

Fireman concentrated on saving the lower portions of the building where the county offices were situated. The high, central clock tower and mansard roofs were lost, and after the fire the building had to be extensively rebuilt. At the time of reconstruction, a fourth floor was added and the main entrance was lowered to ground level.

A touch of late 20th century design was added to the courthouse lawn when Fred Frey's welded sculpture, Caritas, was dedicated in 1978.

Fred Frey's sculpture, Caritas, is a lunch-break companion for a snooze outside the Porter County Courthouse.

Courthouse built	*1883-1885*
Architect	*John C. Cochrane (1833-1887), Chicago*
Construction	*J.W. Wilson*
Cost	*$132,994,*
Population 1990	*128,932*

Cathy Braun and Craig Meyers help keep the burgers hot at the 1985
Popcorn Festival near the Porter County Courthouse.

Posey/Mount Vernon

Mount Vernon was looking for prosperity in the post-Civil War era, and one way of doing that was to attract a railroad. Good transportation could be a key to commercial growth, and so the county issued bonds to raise funds to encourage the construction of a railroad. When that failed, the county found itself with a ready-made fund for a different kind of public work -- a courthouse.

J.A. Vrydagh's design is difficult to classify. Architecture scholar Paul Goeldner describes it as an elaborate example of Italianate design with some timid experimentation in using a low-pitched mansard roof behind gabled projections. The central rotunda, however, is characteristic of a different style altogether, what Goeldner calls "county capitol." A capitol, rather than an Italian villa, is probably what Vrydagh had in mind.

Vrydagh, originally from Belgium, studied at the Louvain School of Fine Arts, and among his other designs in Indiana is East College on the DePauw University campus at Greencastle. The wonderfully restored Victorian building, built in 1869, is a near relative of the Posey County Courthouse.

The brass handrail winding up this staircase in Posey County is a Victorian touch not generally found in Indiana courthouses.

Courthouse built	*1874-1876*
Architect	*J.A. Vrydagh and Levi Clark,*
	Evansville and Terre Haute
Construction	*John McMannomy, Covington*
Cost	*$95,000*
Population 1990	*25,968*

The Posey County Courthouse stands with Victorian tolerance as spectators gather on her lawn to watch the races in Mount Vernon.

Pulaski/Winamac

Judge George Burson of the Pulaski Circuit Court knew in 1893 that the Civil War vintage Pulaski County Courthouse did not comply with Indiana regulations for the protection of government records. Even when it was built in 1862 it probably had been inadequate.

But by 1893 it was almost an embarrassment. Judge Burson, at the request of the commissioners, wrote a report that December essentially condemning the old building. Three days after Christmas, the commissioners accepted his report and ordered the construction of a new courthouse, not to cost more than $50,000, including furniture.

Even for the 1890s, $50,000 was a modest sum for a government building. Tipton County, which was in the process of completing its new courthouse, already had about $170,000 into it. Union County, which had just finished a courthouse, had spent about $110,000. And LaPorte County, not very far to the north, was in the middle of building a courthouse that would eventually cost an astounding $281,000.

What Judge Burson and the commissioners had going for them was A.W. Rush, a Grand Rapids architect eager to exploit an architectural style that could be both impressive and cost effective. The Romanesque, with its massive walls and rough stone facing, could be fancy or plain, but it was never boring. It was fast becoming a popular alternative precisely because it could so easily be adapted to limited budgets. Architects in Iowa and Kansas already had demonstrated the possibility of building interesting courthouses in the Romanesque style for under $30,000. Even in Indiana, W. F. Kaufman had built the Fayette County Courthouse (1890-1891) in Connersville for just over $36,000.

These unusual stone faces --- one smiling and one frowning -- are on either side of the entrance to the Pulaski County Courthouse.

Courthouse built	*1894-1895*
Architect	*A. William & Edwin A. Rush*
	Grand Rapids, Michigan
Construction	*Jordan E. Gibson, Logansport*
Cost	*$42,200*
Population 1990	*12,643*

Chauncey Felker, in his 80s when this photograph was made, stands in front of a wall of memories. They are the photographs of those from Pulaski County who served in the armed forces during World War I. Among those photographs in the courthouse in one of a Private First Class named Chauncey Felker. You will find it on the left side, second row from the bottom. Mr. Felker died August 16, 1988.

Putnam/Greencastle

Before the turn of the century, John Gaddis's courthouses were all built in Illinois and Missouri. He wanted to build the Fulton County Courthouse in 1895 but lost the bid to A. William and Edwin W. Rush of Grand Rapids, Michigan. Gaddis' bid for Putnam County wasn't even a sure thing.

The county was uncertain in 1901 whether the expense of a new building was justified. To settle the question, the state legislature authorized a special election to put the courthouse project on a ballot. The new courthouse won, and Gaddis got the job.

Gaddis designed a simple capitol, drawing on the classical and renaissance ideas that became typical of Indiana courthouses in the early part of the century.

Gaddis also built courthouses at Brazil in Clay County (1912-1914) and at Huntington in Huntington County (1904-1906), all in the same classical renaissance style.

Solomon, deciding the claims of two women for the custody of a child, is depicted in a large mural in the Putnam County Circuit Court.

Courthouse built	*1903-1905*
Architect	*John W. Gaddis (1856-1931),*
	Vincennes
Cost	*$175,729*
Population 1990	*30,315*

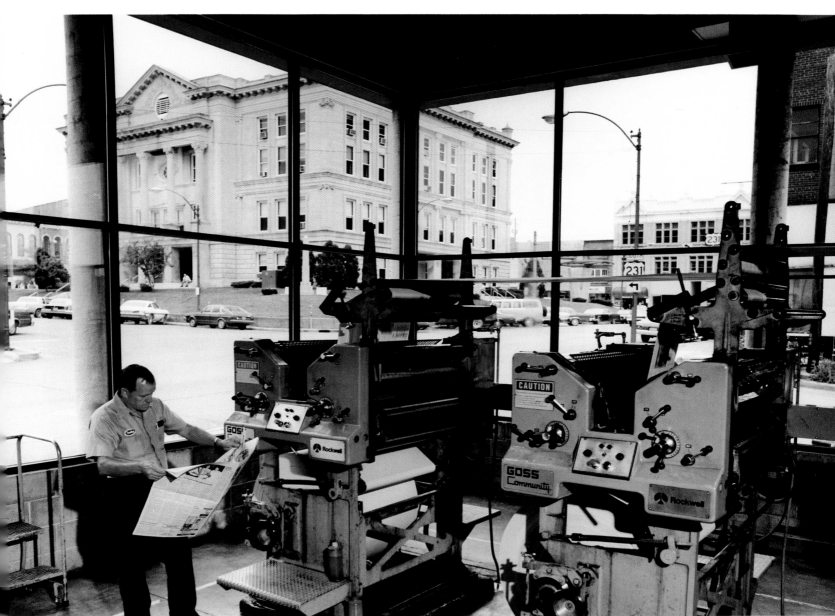

*The Putnam County Courthouse is viewed from the pressroom of the **Greencastle Banner-Graphic.**
Checking the newspaper as the presses run is pressman Harley Crouch.*

Randolph/Winchester

Both the Randolph County Courthouse in Winchester and the earlier Adams County Courthouse (1872-1873) in Decatur were designed by J.C. Johnson, a gifted designer who had been trained as a carpenter and joiner and who taught himself to be an architect.

Both courthouses were originally similar in style with slate, mansard roofs, a central tower and red brick walls ornamented with stone quoins. Both were comparably priced: about $79,000 for Adams County and $73,000 for Randolph County.

By 1875, the old Randolph County Courthouse, originally built in 1828, had long been abandoned and sold by the county. The court met instead in a building on the north side of the square, and the county offices and jail were housed in two brick two-story buildings constructed in 1856.

As early as 1870 the county began a special tax levy to accumulate funds for a courthouse, and by 1875 there was an estimated $35,000 in the fund. For whatever reason, the county apparently used the money in 1875 for expenses and began the building project without a cash surplus. Whether it was because of the curious tax policy or because of genuine misgivings about the courthouse, there was powerful political opposition to construction. Two of the three commissioners failed to be re-elected, and the building was continuously criticized for years as not being fireproof.

Still, it was a wonderful building to look at, even causing one 19th century local historian to wander into rhapsody: "A man might sooner be the architect of that edifice than be President of the United States, or King of England. A President may be an ordinary man, and a king may be a dunce or a madman; but for such a building as that, only genius the most wonderful could conceive, and skill the most consummate could design and execute so beautiful and artistic a structure." J.C. Johnson, a carpenter and self-taught architect, should have blushed in the face of such Victorian praise.

Randolph County's Civil War Monument is 67 feet high. It was designed by A.A. McKain in 1892 and is limestone and granite.

Courthouse built	1875-1877
Architect	*J.C. Johnson, Fremont, Ohio*
Construction	*Aaron G. Campfield, Richmond*
Cost	$73,000
Population 1990	27,148

The painting on the wall of the Randolph County Courthouse depicts the building as it would have appeared before the tower and the mansard roof were removed in 1954.

The Ripley County Courthouse in September is a backdrop for the Versailles Pumpkin Show. The courthouse tower was added in 1932 with money from Florence Grether who wanted it to be a memorial to her husband, Charles.

Ripley/Versailles

In 1860, while a new courthouse was being planned for Ripley County in Versailles, the Odd Fellows suggested a third story be added so they could meet there.

It was considered and dropped, but it wasn't thought to be an inappropriate request. Hoosiers in the 19th century understood courthouses to be public forums for community activity, not just houses of government. It was not uncommon to set aside meeting rooms for civil or fraternal organizations, for religious services or for schools. Many Indiana courthouses still have rooms originally designated for Civil War veterans. Sometimes space in the courthouse would even be leased for commercial enterprises. For example, at Wabash a shoemaker rented rooms in 1845, and at Bluffton two barbers rented basement rooms for shops in 1891.

With the rejection of the Odd Fellows' proposal, the Ripley County Courthouse remained a two-story brick. It was designed by Thomas Pattison in what architecture scholar Paul Goeldner describes as Italianate-classicism rather than Greek Revival, reflecting an approach which allowed fewer rules and greater innovation.

Gen. Morgan reportedly confiscated and smashed the weapons of local citizens on the cornerstone of the new courthouse.

Courthouse built	*1860-1861*
Architect	*Thomas Pattison*
Construction	*James L. Yates*
Cost	*$16,250*
Population 1990	*24,616*

Rush/Rushville

The 19th century was quickly closing when Rush County built its courthouse at Rushville in 1896-1898. The building, designed by A.W. Rush & Son of Grand Rapids, Michigan, was the most elaborate of the architect's three Hoosier courthouses. All of the buildings, whatever the cost, were stately. They included the courthouses at Rochester (1895-1896) and at Winamac (1894-1895) as well as Rushville. Rush had wanted to build courthouses for Hancock and St. Joseph Counties, too, but lost in the bidding.

The Courthouse in Rushville is in a Romanesque style made popular during the late 19th century by Boston's Henry Hobson Richardson. For designers of courthouses, Richardson's work in the 1880s offered specific precedents, especially the Allegheny County Courthouse at Pittsburgh, Pa., the Hampden County Courthouse at Springfield, Mass., and the Minneapolis Municipal Building. Although Richardson died in Brookline, Mass., in 1886, his influence dominated the Midwest during the 1890s, and examples of Richardson-influenced Romanesque courthouses were still being built as late at 1906, a time when most Indiana architects had turned to other styles.

The Romanesque courthouse is typified by rough stonework, huge crux-towers, and wide, heavy, semicircular doorways and shadowy porches.

It is a style that calls up images of abbeys and fortresses, but in the 1890s it was an image already being challenged by a new technology. As the Rushville Courthouse was being completed in 1897, the commissioners learned that their desire for telephones had produced a utility pole directly in front of the north entrance of the building. The pole was removed, but its brief presence marked a passage into a world when architects would not be able to ignore wires and pipes and all the stuff that was to come with progress.

Andrea Reese, on the open stairway of the Rush County Courthouse.

Courthouse built	*1896-1898*
Architect	*A. William & Edwin A. Rush*
	Grand Rapids, Michigan
Construction	*P.H. McCormack & Son, Columbus*
Cost	*$221,941*
Population 1990	*18,129*

Rotunda of Rush County Courthouse.

St. Joseph/South Bend

St. Joseph County has two remaining 19th century courthouses. The oldest is a modified Greek Revival building by John M. Van Osdel of Chicago and dating to 1853-1855. It was moved to a new foundation in 1896 to make way for a new courthouse.

The 1855 courthouse is a national historic landmark and one of the three surviving Greek Revival Courthouses in Indiana. It is the only pre-Civil War public building in the South Bend area, and it is one of the few remaining examples of Van Osdel's work. The Northern Indiana Historical Society occupies the building.

The 1896 courthouse is an early example of the Beaux Arts renaissance style. The commissioners originally asked A.W. Rush of Grand Rapids, Michigan, to prepare a Romanesque design. Rush's courthouses at Winamac, Rochester and Rushville were all in the Richardsonian Romanesque tradition, fashionable a decade earlier but less appealing at the end of the century.

The Commissioners, in a change of heart, dropped Rush, paid him $1,600 in severance and invited six firms to submit plans. They then chose the gracefully academic design submitted by the firm of Shepley, Rutan and Coolidge, which, ironically, was the Boston successor of Henry Hobson Richardson, the architect who inspired Rush's rejected Romanesque designs.

The new courthouse was to be big: 176 feet frontage by 106 feet in depth, with an Indiana limestone exterior and a red tile roof. The original two courtrooms were designed to be 40x60 feet each with 32-foot ceilings. Natural lighting was provided by six, large windows with sills 12 feet from the floor. The high windows were designed to eliminate street noise and distractions. Below the windows was a wainscot of quarter-sawed white oak.

In 1969, South Bend and St. Joseph County completed construction of a $8 million, 14-story City-County Building.

The City-County Building, completed in 1969.

Courthouse built	1853-1855
Architect	John M. Van Osdel, Chicago
Construction	Robert S. Allen, Mishawaka
Cost	$31,482
Courthouse built	1896-1898
Architect	Charles Allerton Coolidge, Boston
Construction	James Stewart & Co., St. Louis
Cost	$240,000
Population 1990	247,052

148

The St. Joseph County Courthouse, completed in 1898.

This is the Scott County Courthouse with its 18-foot monument to William English, a conservative Indiana Democrat who served in the U.S. congress before the Civil War. His sympathies were not with Lincoln, and he returned to Indiana at the outbreak of the war. In 1880 he was the Democrat's United States Vice Presidential candidate. He and his running mate, Winfield Scott Hancock, lost to James Garfield.

Scott/Scottsburg

Curtis Burke remembered Scott County as it was in 1863, a decade before the commissioners paid Andrew Baty $100 to design a new courthouse and jail at Scottsburg.

Burke was a Confederate soldier under General John Hunt Morgan, and Scott County was enemy territory. On July 11, Burke's cavalry unit rode daringly into Lexington, then the county seat, hitched the horses to the courthouse's circular white fence and attacked a nearby candy store.

Burke later wrote: "I got a box of peanuts, some cakes, candy, cove oysters, cheese, etc. We all got as much as we could eat and store about us. It was late when we mounted and took the Vernon road."

Lexington was also the home town of William Haydon English, whose statue now stands before the Scott County Courthouse in Scottsburg.

After the Civil War, it became common in Indiana to erect monuments on courthouse lawns to commemorate wars or heroes. English was a hero. He served as Speaker of the Indiana House of Representatives before he was 30 years old and in 1851 became the secretary of the Indiana Constitutional Convention. In 1852 he was elected to the U.S. Congress as a conservative Democrat but left Washington upon the ascendancy of Lincoln and the outbreak of the Civil War.

He, like many in Scott County, was sympathetic to the Southern cause but opposed to secession. He moved to Indianapolis to become a banker and by 1877 was considered the wealthiest man in Indiana.

Baty's courthouse in Scottsburg is a mostly unadorned brick building. It nevertheless projects a sense of style with its arched windows and front doorway.

Andrew Baty designed Scott County's Courthouse as a simple, two-story brick with a touch of classic stateliness in the roof and windows.

Courthouse built	*1873-1874*
Architect	*Andrew R. Baty*
Construction	*Travis Carter, Seymour*
Cost	*$19,790*
Population 1990	*20,991*

Shelby/Shelbyville

Shelby County's courthouse was built during the Great Depression of the 1930s with a grant from the federal government. It was part of a Work Progress Administration (W.P.A.) effort to stimulate employment and the economy. The federal government contributed $111,600, leaving Shelby County to come up with the rest.

While some Republican Hoosiers in the 1930s complained that W.P.A. stood for "We Poke Along," it meant salvation to many of the unemployed in Indiana. Because almost all W.P.A. money went for wages rather than tools and materials, these public works projects did not compare in efficiency with private construction projects. Still, the workmanship was generally excellent and the overall record was impressive.

Nationally between 1935 and 1941, W.P.A. built nearly 600 airports and built or rebuilt 110,000 public buildings, including the Shelby County Courthouse and the Fountain County Courthouse. It built more than a half-million miles of roads and streets, more than 100,000 bridges, a half-million sewers and a million privies.

The Clerk's Office, Shelby County.

Courthouse built	*1936-1937*
Architect	*D.A. Bohlen and Son*
Construction	*Service Construction Co.*
Cost	*$250,000*
Population 1990	*40,307*

A United States flag and the fall colors of Shelbyville are reflected in the front doors of Shelby County's Courthouse.

The Spencer County Courthouse in Autumn.

Spencer/Rockport

Elmer Dunlap's firm in Indianapolis had a hand in building five Indiana courthouses, including the one at Rockport in Spencer County.

Dunlap was a Bartholomew County native who organized his firm in 1912. By then, however, he had already taken on two important courthouse remodeling jobs -- at Brownstown in Jackson County (1910-1911) and Brookville in Franklin County (1910-1912). In both cases he effectively redesigned old-fashioned, Second Empire buildings into bigger, more modern county capitols in the classical renaissance mode.

Dunlap's other courthouses are those at Delphi in Carroll County (1916-1917) and Petersburg in Pike County (1920-1922). Those two, along with Rockport's Spencer County Courthouse, form a trio of Dunlap courthouses that are closely related. As in Delphi, Dunlap used a stained glass dome over a central rotunda and trimmed the walls with marble. In all three courthouses he kept a basic design, including flattened, interior arches and understated exterior columns.

The Rockport County Courthouse sits in the middle of a part of Lincoln country. Spencer County was Abraham Lincoln's boyhood home from 1816 to 1830. And in 1844 Lincoln returned to Rockport, to the courthouse, to give a speech on behalf of Henry Clay, the Whig presidential candidate.

Over librarian Beverly Symon's shoulder is the Spencer County Courthouse in Rockport.

Courthouse built	*1921*
Architect	*Elmer E. Dunlap, Indianapolis*
Cost	*$275,926*
Population 1990	*19,490*

"Our Lady of the Courthouse" was painted on the ceiling of the Starke County Courthouse at the time of construction in the 1890s.

Starke/Knox

It was this magnificent courthouse in Knox that Richard Pare used as the lead photograph in his book, *Court House*, in 1978. Pare collected photographs of courthouse architecture from all over the nation and was particularly impressed with Indiana's examples of late 19th century structures.

This one in Starke County was designed by the firm of Wing & Mahurin of Fort Wayne and built in 1897-98. It combines Gothic detailing with Richardsonian rock-faced masonry.

The European trained Henry Hodson Richardson established a Romanesque style that was imitated by several Indiana architects who admired his Allegheny County Courthouse in Pittsburgh. For example, one can find examples of the influence of the Richardsonian style at Rochester (1895-1896) by A.W. Rush, at Bluffton (1889-1891) by George Bunting and at Tipton (1893-1894) by Adolf Scherrer.

The Romanesque style was attractive to limited budgets. A plain, large structure could be impressive by itself, and it could be embellished with turrets and towers and gables as the budget would allow. Starke County paid nearly $130,000 for its courthouse, but its neighboring county to the south, Pulaski, built a similar but simpler version a few years earlier for just over $42,000.

The Starke County Courthouse is an excellent example of Richardsonian Romanesque style in Indiana.

Courthouse built	*1897-1898*
Architect	*Wing and Mahurin, Fort Wayne*
Construction	*Caldwell and Drake, Columbus, Ind.*
Cost	*$127,105*
Population 1990	*22,747*

Steuben/Angola

Shortly after the Civil War, Freeborn Patterson designed the brick courthouse in Angola for Steuben County. He built it in the style of Faneuil Hall in Boston, a building famous for its role as a meeting place for patriots during the American Revolution.

The building is distinctive for its arched windows set in tall, sunken panels and for its raking cornice carried by pairs of brackets.

The courthouse was built, mostly on donated land, at the southeast corner of the public square with streets entering the square at the sides rather than at the corners. Such an arrangement is sometimes called a Philadelphia Square and is not typical of Indiana county seats, most of which use a Lancaster Square (streets entering at the sides but with the courthouse in the center of the square) or a Shelbyville Square (streets entering at the corners of the square with the courthouse again in the center).

A good example of a Shelbyville Square is Miami County's courthouse square in Peru and a good example of a Lancaster Square is Orange County's courthouse square in Paoli. The advantage of a Philadelphia Square is that it saves the center of the square for a commons -- a park, parade ground or, as in Angola, the war memorial erected in 1917.

The courthouse at Angola was enlarged in 1937 by adding to the south side at a cost of about $31,000. In 1980-1981 the courthouse was remodeled and restored for about $600,000.

Built shortly after the Civil War, the brick courthouse in Steuben County is distinctive for its arched windows set in tall sunken panels and its curved wooden staircase.

Courthouse built	*1867-1868*
Architect	*Freeborn Patterson*
Construction	*Miles & Holmes, LaPorte*
Cost	*$26,392*
Population 1990	*27,446*

The Steuben County Courthouse sits outside the southeast corner of a Philadelphia square. The center has been reserved for an 85-feet tall war memorial honoring the 1,278 soldiers from the county who served in the Civil War.

Sullivan/Sullivan

John B. Bayard of Vincennes designed both the Sullivan and Vermillion County courthouses during the 1920s. Both were built in the popular classical style and both made generous use of interior marble.

This was Sullivan's third courthouse. The first was a log structure built in 1843, a year after the county was organized. It burned before it was 10 years old and was replaced with a brick courthouse in 1852.

When that one was replaced in 1926, Sullivan, thanks mainly to coal mining, was economically stable and in a better position than some Hoosier counties to rebuild public buildings. Kokomo, for example, reeling from the bankruptcy of the Haynes Automobile Company postponed replacing its courthouse, condemned in 1927, for almost a decade.

Five counties, all in southern Indiana, built during the 1920s: Rockport in Spencer County (1921), Petersburg in Pike County (1920-1922), Corydon in Harrison County (1927-1929), Newport in Vermillion County (1923-1925) and Washington in Daviess County (1928-1929). All except Petersburg and Corydon were built of limestone and all in a similar style. In 1930, Bedford in Lawrence County added one more classical renaissance courthouse.

These six courthouses would mark the end of the classical for Indiana. Never again would courthouses look quite like these. And when Kokomo finally built in 1936, it announced in art deco wonder that a new architectural order was beginning.

The Sullivan County courthouse rotunda.

Courthouse built	*1926*
Architect	*John B. Bayard, Vincennes*
Construction	*Walter R. Heath, Greencastle*
Cost	*$500,000*
Population 1990	*18,993*

nce the 1970s Alma Ridge has made the Sullivan County Courthouse her workplace and her store. She sits by the windows of a basement courthouse room to crochet and to sell her needlework. County courthouses have always been gathering places for people with talent and time.

Switzerland/Vevay

David Dubach probably never saw the building he designed at Vevay in Switzerland County. He is the acknowledged architect only because it was built following the plans he made for the courthouse at Madison in Jefferson County in the mid-1850s.

Dubach's plans were brought to Vevay by Matthew Temperly, who worked with Dubach and was superintendent for the Madison project. The commissioners in Vevay had visited several courthouses in 1862 while trying to decide what they wanted to build. They decided that what they liked best was what Dubach had done, and they adopted the detailed drawings Dubach had prepared for Temperly and which Temperly now was willing to bring to Vevay.

The courthouses in Vevay and Madison might have been exactly alike but the Madison construction firm of Temperly and Woodfield lost the bid for the construction contract. It went instead to John Haly.

At Vevay, Haly used the Dubach drawings but changed the portico columns from Ionic to Corinthian and decreased the pitch of the pediment to a more classical angle. Otherwise he stayed close to the Dubach design that the commissioners liked so much.

The Switzerland County Courthouse.

Courthouse built	*1862-1864*
Architect	*David Dubach*
Construction	*John Haly*
Cost	*$29,745*
Population 1990	*7,738*

A church steeple, a courthouse and a forest outline the skyline of Vevay. Beneath the courthouse is a room that served as a station on the "underground railroad." It was a place of refuge for slaves fleeing the South during the Civil War.

The Tippecanoe County Courthouse towers over the downtown business district of Lafayette.

Tippecanoe/Lafayette

The County commissioners made their final payment on the courthouse at Lafayette in January 1885, and Samuel Clemens is said to have commented that the courthouse "must have struck the taxpayers a very hard blow."

Clemens had been asked his opinion about the courthouse while on a lecture tour that brought him to Lafayette. What he was shown was a building in the high Victorian style. There were a hundred columns, nine statues, a dome with four large clock faces, and a bell built in Baltimore that weighed 3,000 pounds, was tuned to C-sharp and reportedly could be heard 12 miles away.

The building cost about $500,000 and reflected an architecture suitable for a capitol. It has suggestions of the Baroque, Gothic, Georgian, Victorian, Beaux Arts and the Neo-Classical. Its mansard roofs reflect the influence of the then-popular French Second Empire style. But by being eclectic, it manifests a architectural style that deserves its own label. Pau Goeldner in his study of midwestern courthouse calls the building the "epitome of county capitols." I was a time of financial confidence in Lafayette and, a the time it was being built, the Tippecanoe County Courthouse was the largest construction project in the state.

A local architect, Elias Max, built the structure and is usually credited as the designer. However, James Alexander, the construction superintendent probably had considerable input, and it is possible that Max's drawings were based on a courthouse at Quincey, Ill.

At the top of the Tippecanoe County Courthouse dome is a statue of a woman representing Liberty. She is 212 feet above the ground.

Courthouse built	*1881-1884*
Architect	*Elias Max*
Cost	*$500,000*
Population 1990	*130,598*

The Tipton County Courthouse rises in startling contrast to its neighboring homes. It was built in the 1890s and since then has dominated the skyline of Tipton. It was built to be visible from any approach to the county seat.

Tipton/Tipton

Upon the death of architect Edwin May in 1880, Adolph Scherrer stepped in to complete the Indiana State House in Indianapolis, an immense project that lasted until 1888. Five years later Scherrer began construction of the Tipton County Courthouse.

Unlike the classic architecture of the State House, the design for Scherrer's sandstone structure in Tipton was Romanesque, and the building became one of about a dozen extraordinary Romanesque courthouses built during the 1890s that are still being used.

But Scherrer's classical interests are also clearly evident. Despite the steep hip and pyramid roof lines, Scherrer accented the massive building with Doric columns and Corinthian pilasters, uncharacteristic of Romanesque architecture but certainly characteristic of the classical style.

The clock tower, which rises 206 feet to the top of the flagstaff, dominates the Tipton sky line and can be seen for miles across the level Tipton County countryside.

A contestant in the Mr. Pork Loin contest poses for the judges at the Tipton County Pork Festival on the courthouse lawn.

Courthouse built	*1893-1894*
Architect	*Adolf Scherrer*
Construction	*Pierce & Morgan, Indianapolis*
Cost	*$170,988*
Population 1990	*16,119*

Union/Liberty

George W. Bunting had already built at least seven Indiana courthouses when the Union County Commissioners asked him to do another at Liberty in 1890. Only one of his -- at Bluffton (1889-1891) -- was Romanesque, but that is what the commissioners wanted, something in that style and price range.

The contract was for $88,000 for walls, roof and floors. The total cost was to come closer to $130,000, but that was comparable to his Bluffton building, which cost about $120,000.

In 1944, William McMahan described the construction:

"The stone came to Liberty for the new building on flat cars and in huge blocks which were hauled to the site by teams of draft horses. It is believed most of the stone came from a quarry near Cleveland, Ohio, but the first tier above the ground and the uppermost came from an Indiana stone pit.

"...The large stones vary in thickness and are backed up by brick on the inside. The joists are iron of good quality and between these are brick arches, making fire-proof floors and ceilings. The roof supports and rafters also are of iron with narrow strips of wood to which the slate is nailed. The stone eaves are lined with metal of the best quality and the inner trim is of high grade oak."

The massive stone had to be handled carefully and expertly. On the lower floors the stone was lifted and set by a hand windlass with ropes operated on high masts and long booms. Derricks were used for the upper floors and for the 100-foot tower. The stones were pulled into position by horses. McMahan wrote that the horses traveled up Seminary Street to the library corner as they pulled the stone up the side of the building.

But it didn't exactly work right. During July of 1891, after the building was complete and occupied, the tower collapsed. There were no reported injuries, but it took nine months to rebuild.

John Templeton's cabin, built in 1804, was moved here in 1938. Templeton served in the Territorial General Assembly in 1810 and 1811.

Courthouse built	*1890-1891*
Architect	*George W. Bunting (1829-1901),*
	Indianapolis
Construction	*William McKay, Park County, In.*
Cost	*$88,000*
Population 1990	*6,976*

This doorway, with its patina of use and age, opens to the Union County Courthouse.

Vanderburgh/Evansville

Henry Wolters of Louisville designed the old and still remarkable Vanderburgh County Courthouse. The building is what Americans think of as Beaux Arts -- a grandly elaborate Neo-Baroque style. Wolters won the right to design the building as the result of an anonymous competition, somewhat unusual at the time.

The exterior of the courthouse is ornate, with rounded bays capped with domes, porticoes loaded with clusters of columns, and a tall, central lantern. The interior is a profusion of detail, from finely carved woodwork to columned walls, all of which were designed to give an impression of majesty and elegance.

Although it is unlikely the German-born Wolters actually studied in Europe, the influence of the Paris Ecole, where architects were trained to design public buildings, seems evident. also evident is the sophistication of Midwestern limestone carvers before the turn of the century. The building is heavily encrusted with carvings of fruit, flowers and vegetables indigenous to southern Indiana. Franz Englesman of Chicago produced 14 human figures for the building.

The courthouse is no longer used for government offices, but, as in Lake County, houses a variety of specialty shops and public service organizations. There are meeting rooms, a theater and law offices.

County government moved to the new Civic Center Complex in 1969. It has six buildings arranged in a campus style setting on 40 acres. The largest of the buildings is the City-County Safety and Administrative Building. It is a three-story, limestone structure housing all the Evansville and Vanderburgh County offices. The cost of the complex was $25 million.

The Civic Center, constructed in 1969.

Courthouse built	1887-1890
Architect	Henry Wolters (1845-1921), Louisville
Construction	Charles Pearce & Co.
Cost	$466,004
Civic Center built	1969
Cost	$25 million
Population 1990	165,058

(Opposite) This museum courtroom in the old Vanderburgh County Courthouse shows a profusion of architectural detail, from finely carved woodwork to columned walls, all of which was designed to give an impression of majesty and elegance.

Vermillion/Newport

At 1:30 a.m. on May 27, 1923, lightning hit the roof of the southwest corner of Vermillion County Courthouse in Newport. Flames spread rapidly through the building. The loss was estimated at $130,000 with insurance covering about $30,000. Gone were Judge Waits' law library and papers, and gone were all the records of the sheriff, school superintendent, health nurse, surveyor, county agent and highway superintendent. The records of the auditor, treasurer, recorder and clerk were kept in a fireproof vault and were unharmed.

The commissioners selected Halbert Fillinger of nearby Dana as supervising architect for a new courthouse. He then hired John F. Bayard of Vincennes to do the actual drawings.

Fillinger and the commissioners began to visit other courthouses in Indiana to get a sense of what they wanted for Vermillion County. What they decided upon was typical of courthouses in the first quarter of the century: classical, limestone and large.

1924 was the centennial of Vermillion County, but because the new courthouse couldn't be completed in time, the county postponed the centennial celebration to 1925 to coincide with the dedication of the courthouse. On June 11, 1925, the newly elected Indiana governor, Ed Jackson, stood in front of the courthouse as the featured speaker. The courthouse, with its massive stone walls, marble wainscoting and open rotunda, would stand for decades as a symbol of the power of democracy, justice, order and permanence. The governor, with his ties to Indiana's resurgent Ku Klux Klan, would finish office in political disgrace after being indicted on charges of bribery. He was acquitted in 1928, but his political career was left in shambles.

News reporters and camera operators gather in the hallway outside the Circuit Courtroom in the Vermillion County Courthouse.

Courthouse built	*1923-1925*
Architect	*John F. Bayard, Vincennes,*
	and Halbert L. Fillinger, Dana
Construction	*Jasper N. Good, Columbus*
Cost	*$358,707*
Population 1990	*16,773*

Jeffrey Dewers painted the outside wall of the American Legion Post in Newport in 1983.
The Legion is across the street from the Vermillion County Courthouse.

Vigo/Terre Haute

The architecture of the Vigo County Courthouse in Terre Haute, with its mansard roof and iron railings, is a fitting French style for a city with a French name and a French heritage. The style is variously called Second Empire, French Neo-Baroque, or sometimes Stone Quarry because of its massive use of stone. In any case, it was popular in the late 19th century.

The mansard revival in France began in the 1850s with the completion of the New Louvre in Paris. Those buildings influenced architecture in England and America and, by 1865, Isaac Hodgson was designing a mansard roof line on his courthouse in Indiana's Henry County. He used it again in Bartholomew County in 1871 and so did Gordon P. Randall for the Benton County Courthouse in 1874.

So when Samuel Hannaford designed a Second Empire courthouse for Vigo County, he was not a pioneer. But his courthouse was the most expensive of all of them in Indiana.

Hannaford used lots of surface decoration: elaborate window heads, oversized key stones, ornate columns, segmental and triangular pediments, round attic windows. He used a heavy mansard roof and a soaring dome capped with a lantern. The building dominated the Terre Haute skyline. It was huge: 226x277 feet containing 92,335 square feet. There were five floors and the equivalent of four additional stories to the top of the dome.

Hannaford designed the dome to house a local treasure -- a bell purchased in 1879. Inscribed on the bell is this: "By His Will $500 of the Cost of This Bell Were Presented by Francis Vigo, Vigo County, Ind. A.D. 1887." The tale of the bell is that when Vigo died in 1836 he bequeathed to the county $500 for the purchase of a courthouse bell. But Vigo didn't have $500 when he died. All he had of value was a claim for repayment of money he had loaned George Rogers Clark to bring about the capture of Vincennes during the Revolutionary War. It was 1876 before the claim was honored by the federal government.

The Vigo County Courthouse.

Courthouse built	*1884-1888*
Architect	*Samuel Hannaford, Cincinnati*
Construction	*Vigo County*
Cost	*$433,189*
Population 1990	*106,107*

The dome of the Vigo County Courthouse rises above its mansard roof to reach 196 feet from ground level.

Wabash/Wabash

During the 1870s courthouses burned at Nashville, Martinsville, Franklin, Shoals and Wabash. Fire was such a constant fear that it became the most frequent reason cited -- along with claims of inadequate space -- for abandoning ante-bellum courthouses.

Indiana law in the mid-19th century required government records to be stored in fireproof rooms, but not many old courthouses had anything resembling a room that could be called fireproof.

Some, like Wabash, managed to protect records by inconveniently storing them outside the courthouse. Wabash kept them in a brick annex on the north edge of the square. The building housed the sheriff and the surveyor, but most importantly it included a fireproof vault. Fireproof in this case meant a sand buffer between the ceiling and the roof. A bin, filled with eight inches of sand and kept moist by a sprinkling system, provided protection for the contents of the room. Amazingly, it worked.

A devastating fire in Wabash on April 14, 1870 destroyed the courthouse, burned the roof of the annex, but didn't harm the records.

However, the courthouse fire meant that Wabash needed to rebuild.

Construction on a new courthouse began in 1877 after the firm of B.V. Enos & Son was hired to design the building. Enos designed a simple capitol with a tower rising from the center. Some citizens thought it too plain, and so the commissioners ordered the contractor to add minarets to the roof line. Those remained until they were removed in the late 1950s.

No one, of course, designed public buildings with electric lights in the 1870s, so Wabash equipped the courthouse with gas lights and gas generating equipment in the basement. It was efficient and effective. However, within months after the courthouse was completed, the city of Wabash became the first wholly electrically lighted city in the world, beginning with the courthouse dome.

This huge lightbulb was mounted in the tower of the courthouse to demonstrate the potential of electric lighting in 1880.

Courthouse built	1877-1879
Architect	B.V. Enos & Son, Indianapolis
Construction	Lucien & James Gable, Eaton, Ohio
Cost	$96,930
Population 1990	35,069

LIke a gentleman dressed for a dinner party, the Wabash County Courthouse stands above the din of life at its feet.
A county seat is not only a land of deeds and wills and court cases. It is also land of pizza, beer and gasoline.

A tradition in the Warren County Courthouse is to leave the election results on the wall outside the Clerk's and Assessor's offices.

Warren/Williamsport

In 1907, the 1886 courthouse at Williamsport joined the ranks of Indiana courthouses lost to fire. It probably started in the basement and raced up a pine stairway to the attic. In any case, the building was already ablaze when it was discovered about 4:30 a.m. on Sunday morning, January 20.

The building's 155-foot tower collapsed in the blaze, crushing the ceiling of the fireproof vault in the auditor's office beneath it. Records were damaged but most were salvageable. It was a devastating fire, and ironically, the commissioners only a year earlier had reduced insurance coverage from $45,000 to $30,000.

Plans for a new courthouse began immediately. The county hired J.W. Royer to design the building, and the cornerstone was in place by October. The West Lebanon *Gazette* called the new building "an imposing pile of stone and marble." It was imposing. Its $115,000 price tag included massive quartered oak furniture, tile floors and concrete walls with marble wainscoting. The stairways were constructed of iron with marble steps. In case of another fire, there wouldn't be much to burn, except furniture, carpets, window casings and doors.

Royer's idea was to build a county capitol -- classical in taste and topped with a central dome. It was typical of a new style that came with the return of academic classicism after the turn of the century.

The Warren County Courthouse was built with iron staircases and tile floors to help protect against fire.

Courthouse built	*1907-1908*
Architect	*J.W. Royer, Urbana, Illinois*
Construction	*Frank Jahn, Champaign, Illinois*
	and L. N. Cope, Decatur, Illinois
Cost	*$115,000*
Population 1990	*8,176*

This fire hose and iron staircase in the Warrick County Courthouse testifies to a threat that caused many courthouse builders to avoid wooden stairs or floors whenever possible. They preferred iron and marble, tile and plaster.

Warrick/Boonville

Evansville's William J. Harris and Clifford Shopbell designed a building for Warrick County that departed from the styles of the 1890s to capture the basic elegance and simplicity of a classical revival that could produce an almost understated beauty.

It was a fairly modest courthouse for the period, especially since Warrick County was at a turn-of-the-century economic high point during those years. The county was a major midwestern agricultural and mining area. Its wheat was the first prize winner at the 1893 Columbian Exposition and World's Fair at Chicago; its fields of tobacco made it a player in international trade; and its coal mines were producing at an all-time high. Fortunes were being made in Warrick County when the courthouse was built in 1904 at Boonville.

However, the county has been historically associated more with great courage and public service than with great wealth. The county was named for Captain Jacob Warrick, killed at the Battle of Tippecanoe in 1811, and the county seat at Boonville was named for Ratliff Boone (or perhaps in honor of his father, Jesse), an Indian fighter, five-term U.S. Congressman, Lt. Governor and acting Governor of Indiana.

It was Judge John Brackenridge of Warrick County from whom Abraham Lincoln borrowed books as he was growing up, and it was Brackenridge whom Lincoln came to consult when both were Whig party electors in the 1844 presidential elections -- Brackenridge from Indiana and Lincoln from Illinois. Lincoln was stumping for Henry Clay as the Whig presidential candidate that year.

Abraham Lincoln's interest in law began in Warrick County.

Courthouse built	*1904*
Architect	*William J. Harris & Clifford Shopbell*
	Evansville
Cost	*$75,000*
Population 1990	*44,920*

Washington/Salem

Harry P. McDonald graduated from Washington & Lee University in 1870 with a civil engineering degree, and 10 years later, with his brothers, he organized an architectural firm in Louisville, Ky. Six years later, the McDonald brothers had completed one Indiana courthouse at Princeton in Gibson County (1883-1885) and were working on a second one at Salem for Washington County.

By the end of the decade, besides the courthouses at Princeton and Salem, they had courthouses in Illinois at Toledo, Albion and Lawrenceville. Their credits eventually would include the remodeling at Greensburg, another Illinois courthouse at Belleville and the Kansas State Capitol in Topeka.

McDonald was not afraid to try new ideas or to create variations. His clock tower structure is especially unusual. It has a cylindrical belfry with a conical roof set on an octagonal tower that in turn is set on a square tower. Actually this is a recreation of the original. McDonald's clock tower was destroyed by fire in 1934 and had to be rebuilt. The original clock and bell were salvaged and reinstalled.

Sometimes expensive clocks were a matter of immediate controversy. At Rochester, for example, the commissioners were criticized when they spent $1,950 for a clock from E. Howard and Company of Boston. That was about $1,600 over budget. The editor of the Rochester *Sentinel* said that "at that price it ought to strike loud enough to be heard by all the taxpayers who paid for it."

It also was a clock from E. Howard and Company of Boston that the Washington County commissioners bought for their unusual tower in Salem.

The placement of clocks in public buildings has a medieval origin. Here, Lee H. Peugh examines the mechanics of the clock at Salem.

Courthouse built	*1886-1888*
Architect	*Harry, Kenneth and Roy McDonald, Louisville*
Construction	*Crumbo, Melcher, Routh & Co., New Albany and Salem*
Cost	*$72,882*
Population 1990	*23,717*

Rock-faced stone and shadowy porches were thought to be important design element s of Romanesque style courthouses in the 1880s and 1890s.

Wayne/Richmond

After trips to Cleveland, Lima, Findlay and Troy in Ohio, the Wayne County commissioners decided in 1890 to replace the courthouse in Richmond -- a two-story brick building built in the early 1870s -- with a Romanesque courthouse of grand proportions. It would become the largest Romanesque courthouse in Indiana.

The low bid came from Aaron Campfield at $274,425, excluding electrical work. Campfield had built courthouses in Randolph County (1875-1877) and Hamilton County (1878-1879), but neither were as complex nor as large as this job. By the time the project was finished, the total cost probably exceeded $400,000. Architecture scholar Paul Goeldner estimates the actual cost probably was $435,807 -- making it a major public works project of the 1890s.

The Cincinnati architect, James W. McLaughlin, designed the building, and it required 600 car loads of Indiana limestone and 3 million bricks to construct it. The project employed 125 stone cutters on site to cut the stone to fit, and Campfield used steam powered hoists to lift the stone into place.

The interior includes a grand marble staircase and an open well surrounded by open galleries. Wainscoting is marble and the woodwork is oak.

In 1976-1978 the county refurbished the courthouse and completed construction of a new courthouse and administration building just east of the 1893 building. The new building is L-shaped with sloping glass walls and now houses most of the county offices.

Columns inside the Wayne County Courthouse.

Courthouse built	*1890-1893*
Architect	*James W. McLaughlin (1834-1923), Cincinnati*
Construction	*Aaron G. Campfield & Co., Richmond*
Cost	*$287,000*
Population 1990	*71,951*

The Wayne County Courthouse is the largest Romanesque style courthouse in the state and only the second courthouse built at Richmond. The county seat was moved from Centerville to Richmond in 1873.

Wells/Bluffton

On April 5, 1888, Judge Henry B. Sayler issued a court order declaring the Wells County Courthouse to be "unsafe, unsanitary and unfit for use." Judge Sayler thought the 1845 brick building was a disgrace, and he meant to get the court out of it. On May 17, he followed this court order with a declaration that there would be no sessions of court until a new courthouse was built.

The commissioners responded by hiring George W. Bunting of Indianapolis to design a Richardsonian style Romanesque building with four stories and a tower. They liked the Romanesque buildings of Boston's Henry Hobson Richardson, which were massive, stone structures intended to carry a visual message about the permanence and power of government.

Bunting was a popular architect and had already built six Indiana courthouses when the Wells County Commissioners approached him. However, none of those had been built in a Romanesque style. This was a first for Bunting & Son, but it wasn't the last. Even as the Wells County Courthouse was being completed, Bunting contracted to design another Romanesque courthouse for Union County at Liberty. Both courthouses officially opened for public business in 1891.

The cornerstone at Bluffton was set in place amid an atmosphere of celebration. A new courthouse -- often the single most expensive public works project in the history of a county -- was a time for celebration. In Bluffton, the cornerstone was set in place on Aug. 29, 1889. There were speeches and parades and parties all that week. The Methodist, Presbyterian and Christian Churches served hundreds of dinners, and even John Robinson's circus, which had its winter quarters in Peru, came to town.

The judge's bench in Wells County is highlighted by a stained-glass Justice, with scales and sword, and bookcase of the Indiana Code.

Courthouse built	*1889-1891*
Architect	*George W. Bunting (1829-1901), Indianapolis*
Construction	*Christian Boseker, Fort Wayne*
Cost	*$119,879*
Population	*25,948*

The Bluffton Free Street Fair & Wells County Agricultural Exposition fills the streets around the Wells County Courthouse. The day the courthouse was dedicated in 1891, Judge E.R. Wilson remarked that this building was not built because the county needed it, but because someday it would.

David Lottes, a former White County school teacher, is curator of a museum on the second floor of the courthouse. At the upper left on Mr. Lottes wall is a framed print of the courthouse as it would have appeared before it was destroyed in 1974.

White/Monticello

At 5:17 p.m. on April 3, 1974, a tornado swept through Monticello destroying whatever it touched. It ripped the top out of the White County Courthouse, leaving the tower in rubble and the building in ruins.

The commissioners had no choice but to remove what was left of the 1894 Romanesque courthouse designed by LaBelle and French, a Marion firm that also designed the courthouse for Blackford County at Hartford City (1893-1895). In 1975, construction began on a new courthouse designed by Longardner and Associates.

This new White County Courthouse is Monticello's fourth. The first was a wooden frame structure built in 1836. It was simple, but in a time when some courts were still meeting in log buildings, it was relatively sophisticated. The curious thing about that first courthouse was that as it was nearing completion, a violent wind tore it apart. It had to be rebuilt in the summer of 1837.

Eleven years later, the county began construction on a brick courthouse to replace the wooden one. It took three years (1848-1851) to complete because of unexpected delays. For example, city residents believed the area around the courthouse construction site was infected by cholera after the contractor's daughter died from unidentified causes. Construction stopped and county records were moved to the Presbyterian Church. Merchants closed stores and moved families to the country. For two months Monticello was nearly deserted.

The brick courthouse of 1851 was Greek Revival in design and was used for 43 years before being replaced in the 1890s. Eighty years and one tornado later the county salvaged what it could and rebuilt for a fourth time.

The White County Courthouse was rebuilt from the ground up after being destroyed by a 1974 tornado. This carving and the old cornerstone was recovered from the ruins for display on the lawn.

Courthouse built	1975-1976
Architect	*Longardner & Associates, Inc.*
	Indianapolis
Construction	*Black Casteel Construction*
	Corporation, South Bend
Cost	*$2.4 million*
Population 1990	23,265

Whitley/Columbia City

Brentwood Tolan is probably best known in Indiana for his spectacular courthouse designs in Columbia City and Fort Wayne. Tolan and his father, Thomas J., were among Indiana's premier courthouse architects in the late 19th century. In addition to Brentwood's courthouses at Fort Wayne (1897-1900) and Columbia City (1888-1890), their courthouses are at LaPorte (1892-1894), Lagrange (1878-1879), Rockville (1879-1882) and Warsaw (1882-1884). Another courthouse, by Brentwood, at Muncie (1885-1887) was razed in 1966.

During Thomas' lifetime, the firm of Tolan & Son typically designed courthouses in a Second Empire style, characterized by their mansard roofs. After his father's death in 1883, Brentwood built one more Second Empire courthouse at Muncie and then changed styles entirely: a Romanesque courthouse at LaPorte and Beaux Arts courthouses at Columbia City and Fort Wayne.

The Whitley County Courthouse at Columbia City reflects something of the entire Tolan legacy. Its modest details are more consistent with early 20th century styles than with courthouses of the previous 15 years, but the cylindrical projections at the corners reflect the tastes of the 1870s rather than the 1890s or the 1900s. The dome, with its delicate detailing, however, is every bit in tune with the tastes of its period.

Brentwood also added remarkable interior touches to the courthouse, including a translucent floor of glass tiles and massive, windowed doors. Not only were these decorative, they also helped solve a major problem of how to get natural light into so large a building.

In the early 1980s Whitley County spent about $450,000 to clean and repair the exterior and refurbish the interior of the courthouse.

Courthouse built	1888-1890
Architect	Brentwood S. Tolan (1855-1923), Fort Wayne
Construction	Joseph S. Baker, Warsaw
Cost	$148,793
Population 1990	27,651

Brentwood Tolan's glass floor in the Whitley County Courthouse not only added a dramatic touch, but allowed more light into the building

Allen County Courthouse Rotunda

We wish to thank all of the hundreds of people at Indiana's county seats -- court clerks, auditors, commissioners, judges, librarians and county historians-- who provided us with historical and architectural information about the courthouses.

Of particular help was the work of Dr. Paul Goeldner. It was largely his research at Columbia University in the 1960s that brought together dates and construction costs for 19th century midwestern and Texas courthouses.

We would like to thank our colleagues at the Indiana University School of Journalism at Bloomington and Indianapolis, whose support, encouragement and technical assistance was invaluable, especially Trevor Brown, James Brown, Dale Law, Don Baker and Leonard Fischer. We would also like to thank our very able computer consultants from Next Computer, Inc., Rob Francis , and University Computing Services at Indiana University, Liz Hayes.

Others who deserve our deep gratitude and a special mention for their help include: Rose McNeely and Susan Partenheimer of the Indiana Lawyers Auxiliary, Curt Simic of the Indiana University Foundation, James Farmer of the Indiana State Bar Association and Charles and Dorothy Foster.